New to You

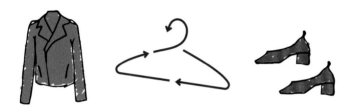

HOW TO BUY, FIX, AND KEEP
SECONDHAND CLOTHING

MELODY FORTIER

QUIRK BOOKS
PHILADELPHIA

Copyright © 2009, 2022 by Melody Fortier

Full Library of Congress Cataloging-in-Publication Data available upon request.

ISBN: 978-1-68369-324-6

Printed in China
Typeset in TheSerif, Century Gothic, and Kabel

Designed by Paige Graff based on a design by Jenny Kraemer
Production management by John J. McGurk

Credits
All photographs courtesy of Melody Fortier except the following: pages 19 (bottom), 37 (top right),
161, 169 (top), Jenny Kraemer; page 13 (bottom three), courtesy of Deborah Burke/AntiqueDress.
com; page 44, courtesy of Manhattan Vintage Clothing Show, from www.jenniferdrue.com; page
157 (top), courtesy of Holly Jenkins-Evans/pastperfectvintage.com.

The publisher wishes to thank The Vintage Connection, Philadelphia Vintage, and Sugarcube for
their participation in the photography on pages 7, 19, 37, 161, and 169.

Quirk Books
215 Church Street
Philadelphia, PA 19106
quirkbooks.com
10 9 8 7 6 5 4 3 2 1

CONTENTS

Introduction

Over the decades the vintage scene has morphed from fashion experiment to established niche. Whether you're new to vintage, or looking for ways to expand an existing vintage wardrobe, there are so many reasons to look to the past for your new favorite garment.

Style: Vintage offers countless style choices; it is a treasure trove for honing a signature look. You will find an endless bounty of fashion prints and colors along with stunning materials, fabulous details, and accessories galore. Each decade of fashion trended toward particular silhouettes, so it's easy to find a cut that complements your body type.

Quality and Value: The quality of most vintage wear is finer than today's off-the-rack garments. Manufacturers of contemporary low- to mid-range clothing have been producing what's called fast fashion for a number of years now, churning out multiple collections each year. These garments are, for all intents and purposes, disposable. On average they start to fall apart after six or seven wearings. Today's lower-end garments might be cheap in price, but you get what you pay for. With vintage you can find quality, well-made clothing and accessories for reasonable prices.

Sustainability: The environmental impact of fast fashion is devastating. Textile manufacturing is often located in water-stressed areas of the world. Combined, the world's textile factories consume a whopping eighty billion liters of water each year, accounting for one-tenth of all industrial water consumption. They also produce extremely toxic wastewater that all too often finds its way into natural waterways.

Two-thirds of garment textiles are synthetic. Synthetic fibers such as polyester are made from petroleum and shed microplastics that contaminate and destroy marine ecosystems. These fibers end up in the food chain and ultimately our own bodies. Studies are finding that microplastics cause a myriad of health issues.

It gets worse. Fashion production accounts for 10 percent of total global carbon emissions, and millions of tons of discarded clothing end up in landfills each year. Plus, the textile industry is notorious for labor exploitation.

Vintage clothing, on the other hand, is all about recycling and sustainability. As long as you know what to watch out for and how to do basic restoration (see chapter 7), your secondhand clothes will last much longer than modern fast fashion, without the destructive effects.

Supporting Small Enterprise: The vast majority of vintage businesses are microbusinesses, and microbusinesses are important. They provide niche products and services that larger businesses deem too unprofitable; they fill up empty storefronts, which helps local economies; they often care about and contribute to their communities in a way larger stores do not; and they are a brighter alternative for those with limited employment choices.

So how does one go about finding, choosing, and buying vintage? That's where this book comes in. *New to You* has all the information you need to become a savvy vintage shopper. You will learn about the different vintage venues—brick-and-mortar stores, online shopping, vintage trade shows—and how to spot a reputable vintage business. This book will also arm you with surefire guidelines to determine if you are getting reasonable value for your money; there are no pricing standards for vintage, and secondhand clothes may have flaws and issues, so without guidance it's hard to know what to pay. You'll learn how to fix some of those flaws (and how to tell when they're fatal and unfixable), as well as how to care for and clean vintage clothing—information that might come in handy for modern clothing, too. Vintage sizes are not the same as today's sizes, and this book will teach you how to determine fit and how to tell when a piece will need to be altered. And of course, you'll learn a lot about fashion trends throughout the decades.

I started wearing and buying vintage in the 1970s. It has been a lifelong passion for me. Coming from a family of seamstresses, I understood good fabric and construction, which gave me a jump start on navigating the vintage market. Still, I made my fair share of unfortunate purchases. Trial and error were my teachers. I want this book to be yours. Happy hunting to you!

Chapter 1

Vintage Defined

VINTAGE IS A LOT OF THINGS. It's classic and stylish. It can be fun and campy. It's even practical and "green." Is it old? Yes, to a certain degree. Is it previously worn? Very often, it is. What, then, differentiates vintage from just plain-old old clothes? Why do celebrities and models proudly grace the red carpet in vintage gowns? Why do major fashion magazines regularly feature vintage wear? Trendsetters and fashionistas consider vintage to be an essential element in their wardrobes. So what then is vintage, really?

Enduring Style

ANY SUBJECT ASSOCIATED WITH FASHION is fraught with intense opinions, and vintage is no different. Definitions vary widely, and some can be quite extreme or rigid. I once read an interview in which a high-end collector insisted that "true" vintage must bear an important designer label. I think it's safe to say that very few people would concur. I challenge anyone who claims that an authentic 1950s circle skirt or 1920s flapper dress is not really vintage, simply for lack of a designer label.

On the opposite end of the spectrum is the broadly accepted idea that vintage is simply "fashions from the past"—anything that's at least twenty years old. As a professional vintage dealer, I'm uncomfortable with such a vague and arbitrary classification. Vintage is not just about age. It has evolved to become a fashion term. It is about essence and style. There is a lot of clothing on the secondary market that is more than two decades old but that I do not include in my personal definition of vintage fashion. As a dealer I pass over volumes of such nondescript clothing. I think we can all agree that not every piece of twenty-year-old double-knit polyester deserves to be resurrected. It may meet the age requirement, but that's about all.

Conversely, there are a few styles that are not very old but that I do consider to be vintage fashion. Especially popular designs often creep back just at the twenty-year mark or even before—see, for instance, the 2010s revival of 1990s grunge. So, the true definition of vintage has something to do with age and quality or appeal, but that's not everything. For me a key concept is what I like to call "Enduring Style." That can mean several things. It can mean classic, like the boxy tweed suit made popular by Chanel, or it can be something innovative, like the sensuous bias cuts that Madeleine Vionnet created in the 1930s. Be they old or not so old, vintage fashions are about styles that are pioneering, classic, or iconic as well as reflective of their era. And although their day may have come and gone, there is renewed interest in wearing them. That, for me, qualifies them as vintage.

Antique and Retro

Occasionally I hear people confuse the terms *vintage* and *antique*. These are really two separate categories, and it's useful to know the difference, especially as you venture into the marketplace. Antique clothing and textiles are generally those that date prior to the 1920s. Some say that one hundred years old is the rule, others think as few as eighty years, to qualify something as "antique." Whichever number you choose, antique clothing is not usually purchased to be worn. As textiles age, they become more fragile and begin to disintegrate. In order to preserve them, they must be stored and handled properly. The beautiful silks and beaded dresses from the 1920s are seldom strong enough to withstand the stress of wear. Although some Victorian and Edwardian garments are still fairly sturdy and will hold up under gentle use, antique textiles are most

Dresses from the early 20th century are sometimes sturdy enough for wear, but you might be better admiring from afar.

often sought as collectors' items or for design reference. Another term for this older category of vintage is *antique-vintage*. Most of today's dealers who sell vintage offer some antique clothing as well and there are a few dealers who specialize in antique textiles exclusively.

Retro is another term used (and confused) with vintage. *Retro* commonly refers to clothing designed to emulate past fashions. In the 1970s, for example, Gunne Sax created retro, Victorian-inspired dresses that became hugely popular. *Retro-vintage* is vintage clothing that evokes an even earlier time than its own. Today, new retro clothing and shoes might emulate anything from 1940s-style pinup dresses to 1990s grunge. Contemporary designers are heavily influenced by vintage styles, and they are always creating retro-inspired collections. Every era is emulated, from Victorian to Mod.

A great deal of clothing described as "retro" today is actually newly produced, but vintage in style. Because it can be intimidating to buy real vintage (hence this book!), people who are interested in the aesthetics alone may turn to these reproduction items instead, because they are easier to source, even though they lack the other benefits of vintage like sustainability and durability (they are generally of modern mass-produced quality). But the same has been true in every era: some new clothing produced at that time has harked back to the past. For the purposes of this book, *retro* will be used to mean vintage clothing or accessories that have been styled after fashions from an even earlier era.

NWT, NOS & Other Initialisms

While shopping for vintage, you're likely to come across a few other terms and funny abbreviations you're unfamiliar with. For example, dealers and online sellers may describe an item as "NWT" (new with tags), "NBW" (never been worn), and "MIB" (mint in box). With vintage, these words mean that the items were previously owned but never used. Similar terms such as *dead stock* or *new old stock* (NOS) refer to recently discovered and resurrected old store inventory that was not sold in its day. Never-worn and dead-stock clothing may not be thought of as secondhand, since it's never seen wear, but it's important *not* to assume that the condition will be just like brand new. Time and the elements always take a toll on textiles. Fading, water damage, creasing, and dust marks are just a few of the conditions that affect even the best-stored pieces. Even if a tag or description indicates that something was never used, make sure you examine it well. When shopping online, read descriptions carefully and ask questions if anything is unclear. You don't want any surprises!

Supply & Demand

THE BUSINESS OF BUYING AND SELLING vintage as street fashion began only around the late 1960s. Before that, textiles and clothing from earlier times were sought by only a handful of people, mostly theater and film costumers, fashion collectors, designers, museum curators, and occasionally the odd eccentric or artistic souls looking to mix vintage into their wardrobe. The average person might rummage through a relative's attic or hit the flea market searching for a costume, but generally it was all considered just "old clothes." Though you might wear them out of thrift, they weren't usually fashion choices. At the end of the '60s, though, there was a rebellion against established fashion, and people looked for alternative modes of dress. They began experimenting with used clothing found in thrift stores and flea markets. It wasn't long before little shops selling pretty or interesting preworn apparel started springing up in cities like San Francisco and New York. In the beginning it wasn't even called *vintage*—I don't recall hearing that term myself until the 1980s—but vintage it was.

The market for vintage fashion has ebbed and flowed over the past five decades, and recently demand has skyrocketed. Vintage permeates popular culture, both in reality and in influence. These days there are outlets for buying vintage everywhere you turn: brick-and-mortar stores in cities and towns, online shops, online auction sites, and even major trade events, such as the Manhattan Vintage Show. Before the advent of such high demand, thrift stores and flea markets were a cheap and plentiful source for vintage. Sadly those days are gone, though you can still find a treasure here and there. And for some of us, the fun is in the hunt!

The Highs & the Lows

Vintage covers nearly a century of fashion. Imagine almost a hundred years' worth of clothing and accessories from every background—mail-order catalogues, home sewn, department stores, boutiques, haute couture. With such an array, you're bound to wonder about quality. You'll surely run into some excellent pieces and some, well, not-so-stunning examples, too.

Vintage runs the gamut, from homemade to midrange to designer.

So how do you know what you're getting? Vintage is usually divided into categories, so let's briefly discuss high-end versus low-end clothing and everything in between. Dealers use this hierarchy to determine prices, so it's important for buyers to understand the various levels. For example, a numbered haute couture dress that's just twenty-five years old can cost many thousands of dollars. Yet a lovely homemade frock from the 1930s may barely fetch $75. They are both vintage, but their differences are like apples and oranges.

High-end versus low-end clothing in the vintage market follows the same conventions and structure as in modern garment making. I'll refer often to these levels, so here is a short list of the most common ones.

- **Haute Couture** The highest quality of vintage clothing. Haute couture was, and continues to be, made to order using the most exclusive fabrics and the finest dressmaking techniques.
- **Couture** A shortened term for haute couture, it is sometimes misused to describe anything from a high-end designer.
- **Ready-to-Wear or Prêt-à-Porter** Clothing that was bought off the rack, not custom made.
- **Better Designer** High-quality limited runs of important designer wear that was bought off the rack. Fabrics tend to be excellent and craftsmanship is superb, sometimes on a par with couture.
- **Budget Designer** Designer-label clothing that is of lesser quality (mostly found after the 1960s) than designer wear or couture. Fabrics and construction vary in quality.
- **Better Name** This term refers to a high-quality manufacturer or a very good but lesser-known designer. It also includes high-end department

store labels, such as Bonwit Teller, Neiman Marcus, and Saks Fifth Avenue. The quality often rivals that of better designer wear.

- **Budget and Midrange** Clothing that was manufactured for lower-priced markets of varying degrees. This category includes mail-order catalogues like Sears as well as low- to midrange department stores. Fabrics are less expensive and construction is adequate but not superior. Despite the diminished quality, designs can be very nice.
- **Dressmaker** Made-to-order clothing created by professional dressmakers. The quality varies but tends to be excellent. Designs are usually derived from popular styles of the day. Very little innovation, as a rule.
- **Home Sewn** Clothing made by nonprofessional home sewers. Quality varies from very poor to excellent.
- **Tailor Made** Clothing made to order by a tailor as opposed to a dressmaker. Tailors tend to limit themselves to making and altering suits and outerwear for men and women. The quality can vary but tends to be excellent. There is usually very little innovation in design, however.

SO, AS YOU CAN SEE, VINTAGE is a bit more complicated than you might've first thought. But with this overview, you now have a good working definition of what vintage is. If I had to sum up my personal definition in one sentence, it would be this: "Fashions from the past that are worthy of resurrection." Determining what is "worthy" is, of course, open to debate and rather subjective—there really are no absolutes when it comes to vintage style. Now let's move on to identifying the varied categories and appreciating their many unique qualities.

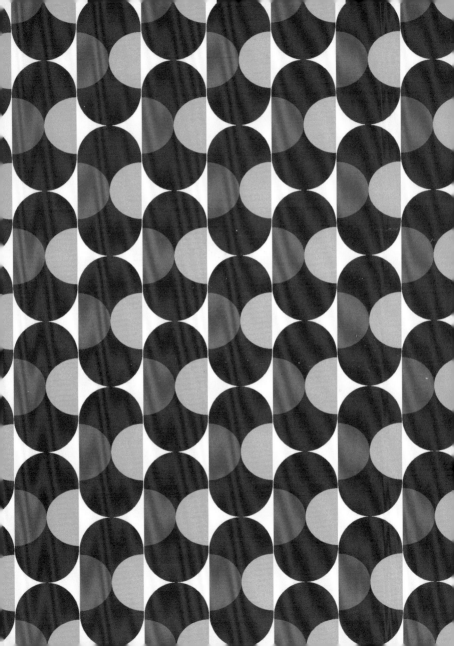

Chapter 2

On the Market

WHY DO YOU ENJOY WEARING clothing from another era? For some it's purely a collector's passion—they want the perfect Madame Grès gown or Dior suit. Others are attracted to the nostalgia the clothes evoke, from postwar femininity to boho chic. A few have a specific goal: Costumers and fashion designers seek authentic pieces on which to base their modern designs. Buying vintage is a form of recycling, an eco-friendly indulgence. Many people shop for vintage because it offers value and a fun, easy way to escape today's disposable culture. So whether you're looking to save the earth or just some cash, vintage offers fabulous quality and a range of categories, from underwear to outerwear.

Unique Chic

VINTAGE MAKES A STATEMENT. One of the greatest complaints I hear from my customers is that modern clothing is so cookie-cutter, and a trip to the local mall quickly reveals that mainstream designs are increasingly generic. The fashion industry has always been highly competitive, and creating for the mass market is not a new phenomenon. But with today's insatiable demand for cheap plentiful goods, manufacturers have had to cut corners. The result is not only diminished quality but a decline in style and innovation. For those who crave a wider palette from which to build a wardrobe, vintage is a fabulous resource.

With all the variety and one-of-a-kind finds, vintage easily fulfills the desire for a signature style. Beautiful classics abound, from little black dresses to smartly tailored suits and timeless coats. You'll discover a wide array of staple separates including pretty blouses, cozy sweaters, and smart skirts. Most women pair these pieces with contemporary basics to create a distinctive style. For those on a funkier fashion quest, vintage is a natural source for experimentation. I love watching the muse at work when imaginative customers cobble together unlikely combinations, such as psychedelic-print tops over jeans or novelty wool blazers or sweaters with today's designer skirts. Celebrities sometimes even turn to vintage gowns for black-tie events because only then can they be certain no one else will walk in wearing the same thing. Nearly every vintage shop will have a healthy selection of event-worthy cocktail or dinner dresses. There's even a flourishing vintage bridal market. And let's not forget accessories—pearl necklaces, rhinestone brooches, fur hats, spiky heels, straw handbags, and on and on. Don't be afraid to mix old and new, funky and traditional, to create a look that's as individual as you are.

Quality & Craftsmanship

Today's ready-to-wear market features scads of clothing made from not-so-great fabrics in varying qualities of cut and construction. Some modern labels are still well made, with fine-quality fabrics, but they are usually very expensive. According to yesteryear's standards, yarns for knitwear should not pill, silks should not wrinkle when crushed, and linens should drape nicely and not feel stiff and wiry. Even some of the old synthetics, such as the Qiana nylons of the late 1960s and '70s, have beautiful qualities not seen today. Many of these old textiles are no longer available or are so prohibitively expensive they can be found only in haute couture. It's amazing to think that much of the vintage you come across has been worn, washed, and stored for *years*, yet it's still perfectly wearable. That's because most women were taught the basics about purchasing quality clothing, and as educated consumers they demanded that manufacturers uphold certain standards if they wanted to stay in business. Today there is no such education, and most modern consumers seem more interested in low price than high quality.

Fortunately, vintage is the last holdout of truly fabulous fabrics you can actually afford. (Unless you can actually afford couture, and if so, lucky

you!) As a vintage shopper, you're sure to encounter luxurious cashmeres that will not pill, cotton sateens that feel like silk, and the most beautiful pure woolens you have ever laid eyes on. You'll see luxurious silk satins and metallic brocades fit for royalty. Clothing makers used all kinds of wonderful laces and eyelets, and you may happen on the real thing—handmade lace that might have taken months or even years to create. Of course not all older textiles are at such a high level, but even everyday vintage clothing tends to be made from a greater variety and higher quality of materials than those seen today.

Vintage also affords fine examples of the dressmaker's art. In the past, much clothing was designed with strategically placed fitting lines that conform nicely to the body's shape, and there are decent seam allowances that permit easy alterations. In fact, before the 1970s, it was common to find

Modern Construction	Resulting Problems	Benefits of Vintage
Tailoring techniques eliminated	Suits and jackets lose shape, or sag over time; linings shift and interfere with how the garment hangs; collars buckle or stick out	Tailoring usually includes under-stitching, hand-rolled collars, steam shaping of shoulders and fitting seams, hand-set linings, high-quality interlinings and underlinings that provide structure

Well-tailored garments hold their shape forever if properly cleaned |
Skimpy over-locked seams	Alteration potential is severely limited; customer must rely on industry standards for fit	Wider seam allowance and free open seams permit easier alterations, greater fitting options
Limited use of fine detail work and quality trims	Fabric prints or generic trims provide most visual interest, resulting in cookie-cutter look	Unique details provide endless variety and give garment character: contrast piping, appliqués and embroideries, intricate hand-applied beadwork, interesting and unusual seam lines, draped and shirred fabrics, beautiful buttons, expensive applied braids and trim, novelty pocket and collar treatments
Lack of handwork and finishing	Garments don't hold up well; fit or hang poorly on the body	Hand finishing and long-lasting touches are impossible to create by machine: cloth-bound buttonholes, crochet lingerie straps, perfectly rolled collars, tacked linings and facings, invisibly shaped hems, hand-rolled edges on sheer/fine materials, sturdy buttons, ribbon waist stays hold waistlines snugly in place

couture-level workmanship in better ready-to-wear clothing. Even budget-line clothing was made well by today's standards. Just as consumers were trained to spot good fabrics, they were equally aware of how to recognize proper fit. To save time and money, today's manufacturers often cut corners by reducing fitting lines. Have you ever noticed how the shoulders of your blazers never seem to fit right? That's because the shoulder dart, which compensates for the roll of the shoulder and allows fabric to lie smoothly, is either improperly placed or absent altogether. Manufacturers also increasingly rely on spandex-infused fabrics to eliminate the need for a range of sizes, opting instead for the catchall S-M-L. But stretch alone will never replace a decent fit. Without proper proportions and well-placed seams, shoulders will strain or droop, necklines will gape, waist- and bustlines will ride up or fall down. Vintage clothing, by contrast, was made in all kinds of sizes to fit many body types: even-numbered sizes or Misses for adult women, odd numbers or junior sizes for adolescents, and half sizes for short curvy figures. With such a range, most people who wear standard or petite modern sizes can find nice-fitting clothing in vintage.

One fairly recent phenomenon is the industry's obsession with *hanger appeal*, a fancy term that means designing a garment to look great on a hanger. From a marketing viewpoint, the idea is brilliant because it's all about stimulating impulse buying. But we all know that a hanger is not a human body, and clothing made to fall neatly on a piece of plastic is not necessarily attractive when worn. Modern designers are under ever-mounting pressure to maintain a competitive edge, so creating clothing that makes women look and feel great is more of a challenge. Here again, vintage rises to the top. Earlier designers concerned themselves exclusively with how something looked on a dress form or a live "fit" model (models with industry standard figures and proportions). But you should keep in mind that a lot of stunning vintage dresses do not look great on a hanger and give very little clue to just how lovely they are once you put them on. A dress cut on the bias tends to droop like a rag, shift dresses can appear totally shapeless (they are anything but!), and full skirts look like nothing special until you put a crinoline underneath. It's the "wearing" that transforms these garments. So don't be afraid to try on something that, at first glance, seems less than stellar hanging on the rack.

Categories of Clothing

NOW LET'S LOOK AT THE DIFFERENT categories of vintage readily available on the market, noting their special attributes and talking a little about how to think about them as you shop.

Coats

Vintage outerwear is definitely the best value for your dollar. The fabrics alone are usually worth more than what you pay for a comparable new garment, and many of the beautiful wools and weaves are no longer available. Cashmere coats top the list. The cashmere used in vintagewear was collected (harmlessly, mind you) from cashmere goats living in the wild in such countries as India and Mongolia. Their modern domesticated counterparts simply do not produce the same fine, silky fur. A cashmere coat from the 1950s is still soft as a kitten and does not pill. Better designers such as Lilli Ann used fantastic mohairs and tweeds imported from Europe, and domestic woolen mills such as Forstmann kept to the highest standards. Aside from the material, the construction of even the most modest vintage coat is usually top-notch, full of fine tailoring techniques. You'd have to pay hundreds of dollars for a new coat made as well. You simply can't go wrong!

Made with better fabrics and superior construction, vintage coats wear amazingly well and look beautiful forever if properly cleaned and stored. Styles tend to be classic, such as Harris tweeds, that blend well with today's casual wardrobes and can easily be updated with trendy accessories. Chic evening coats make a statement, with their elegant lines and luxury details—floor-sweeping opera coats in velvet or brocade, fur-trimmed swing coats, opulent rhinestone buttons, and beautiful linings. Mod '60s and funky '70s outerwear is truly whimsical and fun, especially when the weather is cold and dreary.

Another benefit of coats over other categories of clothing is that the sizing is more forgiving. You can often go up or down in size without ruining the look. Just make sure the fit isn't too tight or that the shoulders aren't too big. Always keep in mind that you'll be wearing layers of clothing underneath.

Dresses

Dresses by far make up the largest category in vintage. And, fortunately for our busy lifestyles, most are easy to wear and care for. The reason they're so plentiful is because until about the 1970s, women wore dresses most of the time. There were styles appropriate for every activity and time of day: dresses for the country or the city, dresses for dinner, for shopping, for housework, for gardening. There were beach dresses and travel dresses, evening and ball dresses. Some women of a "certain class" might change outfits four or five times a day! Even the middle-class homemaker was known to change into a fresh frock for the family dinner. We're certainly not so formal today, but it may be refreshing to sometimes put aside the jeans and don a pretty dress instead.

Expert Tip

Finding the Perfect Vintage Dress

WENDY RADICK
OWNER, KITTY GIRL VINTAGE

If you're shopping online for that special soirée dress, here are a few tips to help in your quest. First, take your measurements or have a professional take them for you (see chapter 5, "Sizing It Up"). The chance of finding the perfect dress with the perfect fit is not impossible, and you definitely want to be prepared. Make sure you note any unusual measurements—for example, a larger midriff or longer torso.

Next, make sure you know a good seamstress who can make minor alterations to give your dress just the right fit. Sometimes a simple change of hemline or sleeve will do the trick. And last, make sure you can return the item. Return policies on vintage clothing vary from site to site, but most owners want their customers to be satisfied. Some may send more than one dress "on approval," meaning that you buy only what you want and return the rest. You never know—you might just end up with more than one perfect vintage dress!

Cotton (or blended) shirt dresses from the 1950s and '60s are hugely popular with vintage shoppers. These everyday frocks may have full or straight skirts, and they come in an endless variety of pretty prints and solid colors. One- and two-piece knit dresses have a different look, depending on the decade. The 1940s and '50s featured beautiful bouclé wool knit sets with straight or faux pleated skirts and matching cropped pullover tops. I come across many that are plain, but some have light embellishments—a bit of beading on the collar or shoulder, a couple petite rhinestone buttons—though in general the details are not overly fancy. Simple 1960s shifts in monochromatic double-knit fabrics are a perfect canvas for expressing personal style. The wool knits are nicest, but you can find some very good synthetics as well. The '70s are known for their knit and jersey dresses, with styles ranging from youthful empire and baby-doll types to the forgiving wrap dress (thank you, Diane Von Furstenberg). Knit dresses tend to look ho-hum on the hanger, so they're easy to overlook—don't make that mistake! A well-cut knit dress can be the most flattering garment you own. Try a few on.

A bit more formal are tailored dresses that range in style depending on the decade. I am quite fond of the solid rayon crepes from the 1940s and early '50s; with navy blue and black the most common, these dresses are the perfect background for accessories. They often have long sleeves and higher necks that could look prudish were it not for the way the material defines and skims the figure, coming in at the waist and curving over the hips. Shoulder lines are strong and sometimes have a decorative drape or swag. Contrasting collars and cuffs are occasional embellishments. Gabardine dresses are always smart looking and wear exceptionally well, especially the wool ones. Some of the wools, like those from the '60s, are thick and textured. Lighter-weight wool dresses are nice for seasonal transitions and often come in neutral colors. These fabrics do not need to be cleaned with each wearing; see the "Condition & Care" chapter for advice on keeping clothing fresh longer between cleanings.

Vintage party and formal wear has a large and growing market. Proms and weddings, cocktail parties, and even black-tie events (think Oscars) are often sprinkled with vintage glam. Being assured of wearing a one-of-a-kind is a major draw, but so are the luxury fabrics and glamorous styles. Diaphanous chiffons from the 1920s (for those with deep pockets), sultry bias cuts from the '30s, elegant beaded jackets and floor-length gowns from the '40s, frothy '50s tulle gowns and sexy "wiggle" dresses, clingy '70s Halston gowns, pouf dresses from the '80s—all make for devastating cocktail wear.

Separates

Next on the list: sweaters and blouses, skirts and pants—in short, the staples of today's casual wardrobes. If you're looking for a bit of flair, then mixing modern with a hint of vintage is the way to go. Vintage sweaters are especially easy to wear and are almost always fully fashioned, meaning that they were knit all in one, not sewn together from pieces, which makes them hang and wear nicely. Without bulky seams, they form one smooth line and are much more flattering than today's styles. Cashmere sweaters are well worth the extra money. Older cashmere is superior to modern varieties and will not pill or wrinkle. If you keep the moths away and wash gently by hand, they should last forever. Those by Dalton are my favorite, but beaded '50s cardigans, cozy '60s mohairs, '70s novelty knits, and '80s oversizeds are all the rage among many of my customers.

From underwear to outerwear, vintage offers endless variety and styles.

Smoothie
CONTROLEUR ®

The STROUSE, ADLER CO.

FIBER CONTENT
ON REVERSE SIDE

STYLE 8136   SIZE 28

Beautifully tailored jackets and blazers often boast superior fabrics and design details like novelty buttons, fancy pocket treatments, and bracelet-length sleeves. I especially like hand-bound buttonholes. Pretty details were important "back in the day," and today you'll see some of these techniques only in couture. You can choose from several silhouettes, from the hour-glass shapes of 1940s padded shoulders and fitted waists to the boxy cropped version of the later 1950s and '60s. These work well on a thicker midriff, particularly if you have narrow hips. Vintage skirts are plentiful, too. One of most requested styles is the full, gathered, or circle skirts from the 1950s. These range from casual cottons and felts to dressy taffetas and laces; the dressy ones are a wonderful alternative to a party dress, especially when paired with an elegant fitted top and high heel. Skinny pencil skirts, easy

wraparounds, and Mod maxi prints (if you dare) are all abundantly available and fun to try. Again, the key is to keep the rest of the outfit modern except maybe a vintage accessory here or there.

For a quick transformation of any outfit, try a little vintage top. During midcentury, sheer nylon blouses were tremendously popular, and you can find versions with tucks and pleats, delicate lace, and little rhinestone buttons. "Camp" blouses (boxy styles with short fold-up sleeves and small collars) come in fun novelty prints, pretty florals, and classic solids. The better ones are made from the finest cottons as soft as silk; I am fond of the Gabey brand.

And let's not forget the skinny polyester and nylon shirts from the '70s, with their oversized pointy collars and their psychedelic and op art prints. Huk-a-Poo produced exceptional examples, and their fabrics are nice and silky. Bohemian and peasant-inspired looks can be found from nearly every decade, but the trend exploded with the hippie movement in the later '60s and '70s. Authentic hippie clothing has become very desirable—even more so if it is patched or embroidered by the original owner.

Women's pants were not plentiful until the 1970s, so early styles are relatively scarce. There is less of a market right now for vintage pants because they fit so differently than modern ones. They often have very high waists, for example, which some women find unflattering. Yet don't dismiss them out of hand. They're an untapped source and can be quite reasonably priced. Wide-legged bell bottoms in fabulous prints and bold plaids, sailor-style trousers with button fronts, and flowing palazzo pants are a few of the types you may encounter. Even if the cut falls out of your comfort zone, try them on anyway. You just might be surprised.

Lingerie

This is a category that I am particularly partial to. Today beautiful lingerie is a costly indulgence mostly reserved for romantic occasions. But there was a time when women wore beautiful underthings every day, just for themselves. In Victorian times, petticoats, camisoles, and chemises were often generously trimmed with fine laces, embroideries, and ribbons. Stunning examples made from sturdy cotton appear regularly on the vintage market and are one of the few antique textiles still practical to wear. No longer relegated to underwear, these oh-so-feminine pieces can easily be layered with today's trends. My customers clamor for sleek bias-cut boudoir gowns from the 1930s embellished with delicate embroidery and wisps of lace; they love the way the fabric flows like liquid over the body. Slips are the most abundant types of lingerie available. They're still perfectly functional, smoothing out the lines under thin fabrics or jersey knits, and make nice sleepwear, too. So much prettier than sweats! Loungewear is also easy to find: pretty robes, sexy peignoir sets, and frilly negligees. Some of the better names to look for are Vanity Fair, Barbizon, and Van Raalte. Intimate apparel includes bras, corsets, and girdles whose main function was to shape the figure to the prevailing silhouette. Early bras, for example, were created to minimize the bosom, whereas those from the 1950s exaggerated the bustline. You can find a wide range of vintage dainties on the market, and all are generally very pretty and exceptionally well made.

Purchasing Power

NOW THAT YOU KNOW WHAT'S ON THE MARKET, where do you find it? The vintage marketplace is varied and virtual. You can often shop right from the comfort of your own home thanks to online storefronts and auction sites. For those in more rural areas, the web is heaven-sent (although note that some of the best vintage shopping is available off the beaten track and far from the big cities). Here are a few tips for navigating the wide world of vintage shopping.

Flea Markets, Thrifts & Their Ilk

It used to be that secondary markets were the best places to unearth bargains—and you can definitely still find some great deals and amazing pieces in these places. But the recent surge in the popularity of vintage has caused some flea-market vendors and thrift-store owners to raise prices on any older clothing and accessories, often without really knowing what's what as far as value, quality, authenticity, and rarity are concerned. So be careful not to overpay. Recently, I visited a second-hand store that was selling several fake designer bags from the '80s, with fairly high prices. The clerk justified the prices because the bags were vintage. If they had been genuine they would have been a steal, but for fakes they were way overpriced. Just because it's old doesn't make it good.

But generally speaking, at flea markets, yard sales, and thrift stores you'll find the lowest end of the price scale. If the price seems too high, it probably is. These places are able to charge less because they have little overhead and/or they sell merchandise that has been donated. But there are always tradeoffs when you opt for the cheapest route. It can get pretty down and dirty rummaging through racks and piles of not-always-fresh second-hand clothing hoping to find the vintage treasures. However, if you approach these venues with a keen eye and some solid know-how, there *are* some great bargains to be found. I once bought a Ceil Chapman dress at a flea market for $5! Needless to say, I was on cloud nine for days.

When you shop the "thrifts" you will likely not be dealing with professional dealers, so you're on your own with assessing the pieces offered for sale. You should expect flaws and the need for cleaning, so keep in mind what those might cost you in money or effort. In addition, unless there's a space to try things on, you'll need to calculate fit by means of measurements, both your own and those of the garment. I walk you step-by-step through the process of taking your own measurements in chapter 5, "Sizing It Up"; be sure to bring them with you, along with a tape measure.

Vintage Shops & Other Venues

Retail stores are probably the most fun places to shop—what with their racks crammed with endless variety, their enthusiastic owners full of advice and recommendations, and their dressing rooms for ensuring a good fit. Although store prices are much higher than those at flea markets and thrift stores, the owners work tirelessly to acquire a top-notch selection. That's not easy when you're dealing with a hundred years of fashion! Most dealers also put effort into cleaning and mending their vintage so that it's ready to wear. They are usually extremely knowledgeable and can advise you on everything from fit to era. Depending on the shop's location, the prices will range from modest to sky high. (What's the old saying? Location, location, location . . .) That's usually because, in major urban areas, the overhead is exorbitant and the demand will be high, so naturally the owners charge top dollar. Travel farther away from the hot spots, though, and prices plummet. The out-of-the-way stores may be harder to get to, but in savings and selection they're well worth the trip. They may not be well advertised, so be sure to ask around. Whenever I go on a road trip, I ask local folks if there are any vintage clothing stores in the area. Sometimes I even call the local chamber of commerce.

Vintage shows are also a fantastic place to find the most amazing vintage, but they are not cheap. Yet despite the entrance fees and higher prices, they are still one of my favorite places to shop for vintage. Dealers reserve their best materials for these events, so everywhere you look you'll see the cream of the crop. It can be overwhelming, so you may want to have a strategy and only visit dealers offering what you're searching for. My suggestion is to approach a show the same way you would any occasional splurge or indulgence. It's always good to keep a budget in mind, but be flexible. If you find something extraordinary, you might want to raise your bar a bit. I once found a 1930s brooch at a show and it cost quite a bit more than I usually spend. It was stunning and I decided I had to have it. I receive compliments every time I wear it, and it has become one of my absolute favorite pieces. The moral of the story: Sometimes it's better to buy than to live with the regret.

Venues like the Manhattan Vintage Clothing Show offer dozens of dealers under one roof.

Auctions are yet another venue for buying vintage. There are basically two types: actual auction houses where you physically go to view and bid and online auctions like eBay. Whichever you choose, know that auction prices are always volatile. If two people are determined to have the same item, the price can well exceed its true value. On the other hand, lack of interest can result in some good bargains. At a house auction you can preview items before bidding, but usually you can't try them on. Returns are not accepted, so bring your measurements and a tape measure. Auction houses also charge what is called a buyer's premium. This means that you will be paying the auctioneers a percentage over and above the closing bid. This can be as high as 20 percent, so beware. A calculator might come in handy.

Shopping Online

Even if you do live in an area where stores are plentiful, they can be very expensive, with the cheaper ones offering picked-over merchandise. Fortunately, the demand for vintage has sparked a slew of online sources. The three major venues are the dedicated vintage website, mini-shops in virtual malls like Ruby Lane or Etsy, and online auctions.

If you shop at an established, trustworthy online store or mini-shop, you will be paying "internet prices"; basically, reputable sites with nice merchandise tend to price on the higher side. Aside from all the work that goes into procuring decent vintage, each item must be photographed and accurately described, with proper measurements and a detailed condition report. This extra effort is reflected in the pricing. Shipping costs also need to be factored in. Boutique online dealers appreciate that their customers are paying well, so they try to offer exceptional merchandise along with very good service. Although you won't necessarily find bargains at these sites, you do get your money's worth, especially when it comes to convenience. And if you're looking for something specific, chances are you'll find it on one of these online sites. Plus, the prices are not always higher than those in the shops; in fact, if you live in an expensive urban area, they might actually be lower.

Earlier I mentioned vintage offered by auction houses, and now I'll touch on online auction sites. On the internet, you must rely on descriptions and pictures since you can't preview the item in person. Take the time to ask specific questions about fit and condition and check if there is a return policy and what the terms are. The best way to avoid overpaying at any auction is to have a ceiling price in mind, and do not exceed it, even in the excitement of the moment. Be thorough and learn what you can ahead of time. That way there will be no disappointing surprises if you do win.

THE VINTAGE MARKET OFFERS ALL the same variety as your local mall or chic boutique, and you should expect to pay for quality and rarity. The value of vintage is not necessarily a lower price, it's better quality and unique style. You may be able to find treasures for pennies at the flea markets or thrift shops, but you'll have to kiss a lot of frogs first. The advantage of shopping with dealers in shops and online is that they've done all the work for you, offering an edited selection of quality items that are ready to wear. It's usually worth the expense.

My best advice is to get to the shops, peruse the selections, and try things on. Keep an open mind and let the creativity flow. Ask the shopkeeper for help. Most of us just love to dress people and have seen what works and what doesn't. Use us as a resource and you won't be disappointed. And, most of all, have fun!

Chapter 3

Styles of the Times

TO BE A SAVVY VINTAGE clothing shopper, you should know about the evolution of styles throughout fashion history. Eventually you'll train your eye to identify signature looks from the past, and then you'll be able to better predict how the clothing will fit and what will work best for your body type. You'll also be able to spot the differences between an original vintage item and a retro piece (vintage-inspired clothing), an important distinction that affects price, care, and storage. In short, you'll know what you're buying. Most of all, studying fashion is fascinating and will, I hope, inspire an appreciation for each piece of vintage you add to your wardrobe.

Dressing by Decade

TODAY'S VINTAGE MARKET ENCOMPASSES MORE THAN 100 years of popular style—everything from breath-stealing corsets, swingy flapper frocks, and gossamer tea dresses to beaded cashmere cardigans, floor-sweeping maxi skirts, and, well, breath-stealing corsets! As you shop for vintage clothing and accessories, you'll probably notice several things that differ from today's garments, like cut and quality as well as materials and embellishments. One difference sure to stand out is the formality of vintage clothing, not just in evening attire but daywear, too. Although many of the clothes that have survived were reserved for special occasions and are therefore of better quality, it's no secret that people used to dress much more formally than we do today.

The twentieth century saw amazing changes in culture, technology, and of course fashion. In this chapter we'll look at an overview of the various eras and their styles, beginning with the turn of the last century. Certainly such a condensed timeline cannot cover every style that occurred within those decades, nor can it consider the many tiers of societal dress. And not to be overlooked are accessories, an integral part of fashion that help define an era's special look. Accessories are abundant in the marketplace and can be an easy, fun way to personalize your individual look, so we'll examine a few major trends. All this information will help you identify major fashion milestones and recognize periods. So let's begin our brief history lesson.

1800s through the 1920s

The periods from the 1800s to 1910 are referred to first as Victorian and then Edwardian, terms that are linked to historical events in England (and its ruling monarchies) but that have come to apply to fashion history as well. For many of us, these words call to mind ruffles and lace, parasols and afternoon tea. *Victorian* in particular is often used as a general catchall to describe any "antique" style that is frilly, fussy, and full of lace. In the field of vintage, however, *Victorian* (early, mid-, and late) and *Edwardian* refer to specific eras with their corresponding styles, not a generic look. To confuse things even further, in France the period from the latter 1800s through 1914 is called la belle époque. We will be concerning ourselves with styles from the 1900s through the teens, which, for the sake of simplicity, I will refer to as *early twentieth century*.

Evolution in fashion often reflects society in general, and the garments from the turn of the last century signal important changes in women's status. As the "gentler" sex was actively promoting the suffrage movement or taking up new forms of exercise, they welcomed clothing that was less voluminous and cumbersome than prior fashions. Gone are hoop skirts, endless crinolines, and awkward bustles in favor of a straighter silhouette. Two-piece dressing, composed of a bodice and skirt, gained popularity alongside the one-piece shirtwaist dress. Women's attire was generously decorated with delicate laces and intricate embroideries. The preferred textiles were lighter weight, often sheer: cotton lawn and voile, lightweight silks, and fine woolens. Underneath it all was the corset, the mainstay of women's clothing for centuries. At this time a new type was introduced, the S-curve corset, whose complicated, rigidly boned structure caused a woman's chest to be thrust out, the hips forced back, and the lower back bent into a pronounced curve, creating the prominent bust and cinched waist typical of the era. Other undergarments were elaborately embellished— petticoats were garnished with tucks and ruffles, lace, and embroidery, and corset covers and camisoles were beautifully detailed. These pieces can still be found today in wearable condition, and they make perfectly charming outerwear.

The war-torn teens were a difficult decade for many worldwide, and fashion weathered the storm of changing lifestyles. As women got down to the business of working in factories, delivering mail, and nursing soldiers, they needed more freedom of movement. Hemlines began rising, eventually reaching midcalf, and waistlines were repositioned higher. Sturdy practical cottons, linens, and woolens found favor over more delicate fabrics (except for special-occasion clothing), and decoration included pleating and floating panels, strategically placed buttons, wide collars, and passementerie (trimming) of applied cord. Even more important, the business of foundation wear was being turned on its head. The corset was slowly abandoned, and it was during this time that the brassiere was invented.

The 1920s ushered in an era of jubilance and optimism, and the U.S. economy thrived. People were eager to let loose—it wasn't called the Roaring Twenties for nothing—and they sought out glamorous clothes to celebrate in. Flapper style, perhaps more than any other in history, truly reflected the era, with its new liberalism, cultural exchanges, and shifting sexual norms. Although the word *flapper* had been coined earlier to describe brash young women who flouted society's rules, it became widely used during this decade. The flapper dressed shockingly, with fringy hemlines on sleeveless, sliplike dresses that enabled her to swing and sway provocatively to the emerging forms of jazz music and energetic dances like the Charleston. She also lopped off her tresses into the now-iconic bob, and in a few short years women of all ages were hiking their hair as well as their hemlines, which soon rose all the way to the knee (scandalous!). Also fashionable were dropped waistlines, pleated skirts, silk anything, and fur-trimmed coats.

Accessories

During each decade, a few shoe styles rise to the top of the fashion heap, becoming emblematic of their time. For the turn of the last century, the lace-up boot is a perfect example. The era also favored fine pumps of leather and fabric, many sporting a squat Louis-style heel. Sturdier, work-a-day and walking shoes were also plentiful, some with laces, others with side-button straps. You'll notice that, in general, footwear from these early decades is narrow with a pointed toe (making them a bit difficult to wear today). In the 1920s, the toe box became more rounded and a little less slim. Strap shoes and pumps with a Louis heel remained popular, but boots generally fell out of vogue except as outdoor wear. Dress pumps featured beads and embroidery, fancy buckles, exotic leathers, and rich brocades.

The century's early hats were true feats of millinery splendor. Flamboyant brims created the perfect canvas for creative embellishment: crowns swathed in silk, velvet, netting, or lace, and exotic plumage reigned supreme. Also popular were simple straw hats, a more practical alternative for the athletic woman enjoying outdoor pursuits. The first cloche hats appeared in the teens, and today these bell-shaped, close-fitting chapeaus are synonymous with flapper style. They signaled a trend for softly constructed fabric hats embellished with nothing more than intricate folds.

Costume jewelry proliferated beginning in the early 1900s, thanks to developments in mass production, which created a wealth of ornate pendant watches, cameos and lockets, and buckles and brooches, many featuring swirling art-nouveau or plant-based motifs. Delicately beaded or mesh wristlet handbags made for easy transport on evenings out, and larger fabric satchels were most often reserved for travel. The art deco movement that appeared in the 1920s heavily influenced jewelry and handbags, lending them a streamlined, geometric look evocative of society's love affair with the new "machine age." Iconic of the flapper age is the long strand of beads or pearls, but bracelets and ear bobs were also abundant. For evening, women wore tiaralike headpieces or bandeau sashes around the forehead, often with a bejeweled plume. So chic!

1930s & 1940s

The Roaring Twenties came to a screeching halt with the crash of the U.S. stock market in 1929. Fashion changed seemingly overnight as women sought a return to the comfort and familiarity of modest femininity. By 1932 the hemline had once again fallen to just above the ankle. The waistline returned to its natural place, and although the overall look remained willowy there was more emphasis on an hourglass figure. It was also in the 1930s that the bias cut—fabric cut on a diagonal—became popular, allowing clothing to fall in gentle folds and drapes that gracefully mold to the body. Sensual but never vulgar, this treatment soon permeated much of fashion throughout the entire decade. On the other side of the coin, Depression-era women demanded good-quality, durable clothing that would not fall quickly out of fashion. They were amazingly innovative, restyling older garments or crafting dresses from the printed fabric of flour and seed sacks. This practice became so popular that the flour and seed companies began offering variations of prints in an effort to entice sales. As a counterpoint to the era's frugality, clothing boasted incredibly inventive fitting lines and a new fullness, the result of godets (insets of cloth in a seam), decorative yokes, and asymmetrical pleats, not to mention an endless variety of pocket styles and treatments.

During the Depression, women had looked to soft femininity to lighten the economic hardships, and the silhouettes evolved only slightly. The advent of war changed everything, boosting the 1940s economy but also straining resources: Many of the raw materials used in the garment industry were needed for the war effort, including textiles and ingredients in commercial dyes, resulting in a more subdued palette. In 1943 the U.S. government placed limits on fabric amounts for clothing. One quote from a fashion magazine notes: "The silhouette for 1943 is slim, pillar-like, with not a bit of extra material that could be used by Uncle Sam." Other restrictions prohibited oversized sleeves, decorative trims, patch pockets, hoods—just about anything that required excess fabric. Rayon substituted for wool and silk and was woven into gabardines and crepes.

Wartime silhouettes were neat and trim. Hemlines rose to just below the knee, and skirts were cut slim over the hip, with just a bit of flare. Bodices were fitted, sleeves were simple. Suits were popular, with shorter nipped-waist jackets and peplums to soften austere lines, and padded shoulders became de rigueur. Especially popular were knee-length dresses in pretty rayon prints, though casual wear and sportswear grew in popularity. Fashion separates were quickly embraced by old and young alike: Skirts and sweaters, tailored blouses, jumpers and jerkins were all smart-looking and easy. Trousers were being worn increasingly, and blue jeans, once reserved for farm or factory, became a fad. For formal occasions, long evening skirts and beaded jackets were popular, though the look turned more modest, with higher necklines and covered shoulders.

By the end of the 1940s styles were once again changing dramatically. Enter the ideal of woman as homemaker, an image thoroughly embraced by popular culture. Contemporary magazine ads show her sporting belted shirtwaist dresses and frilly aprons. Her hair was perfectly coiffed and she never left the house without hat and gloves. For a trip into town she might wear a smart suit with fitted jacket and long skirt. In 1947 Christian Dior released his first couture collection, which rocked the fashion world and introduced soft shoulders and tiny waists set off by voluminous skirts. The tide had turned and the "New Look" became the inspiration for what was to come.

Accessories

With tight budgets in the 1930s came an increased reliance on accessories to change up an outfit. Women dusted off their dressmaking skills to whip up removable collars and cuffs, and they cleverly crafted homemade jewelry as well. Bits of fabric and felt were fashioned into sweet corsages; beads, apple seeds, and corks were strung into textural necklaces; and scraps of wood were carved and painted to create one-of-a-kind brooches. In the 1940s costume jewelry sometimes reached impressive proportions. Oversized brooches and cuff bracelets were a fun foil for simple suits and plain rayon dresses.

Enormously popular was jewelry made from the recently invented plastic Bakelite. Sturdy and durable, Bakelite could be created in myriad bright colors and carved into wonderful shapes. Today pieces such as bangles and brooches are highly collectible.

The 1930s saw Hollywood-inspired extravagance, perhaps the result of increased movie-going, which was the preferred pastime for cash-conscious Depression-era families. Shoe styles evolved to include more details: cutouts and fancy straps, huarache-style woven leathers, dainty bows, and elaborate punchwork. With wartime restrictions on leather in the 1940s, new materials such as cloth, plastic, and straw were used to make shoes, belts, and handbags. Exotic skins such as crocodile and lizard also gained popularity for accessories. Peep-toe shoes and platforms became the rage and are one of the most-recognized trends from this era.

Hats continued to be whimsical throughout the 1930s and '40s, providing opportunity for indulgence. The era opens with the full cloche covering the whole head, though by 1932 it had shrunk down to more of a close-fitting cap. Milliners created all types of smart little hats, and it was the vogue to tilt them down over one brow at a rakish angle. The fedora style for women also became popular (thank you, Marlene Dietrich). Persian lamb and exotic animal furs were common materials for hats and coordinating matching oversized muffs.

1950s & 1960s

By the beginning of the 1950s, society was well on its way to unabashed preoccupation with style. Paris couturiers were flexing their creative muscles, producing one breathtaking season after another. As much as ten yards of expensive fabric might go into the making of one dress—swirls of slipper satins and rich brocades, frothy organzas, cotton sateens, and rich tweeds in vivid colors.

Ball gowns and cocktail dresses aside, American casual wear and sportswear still made up the larger portion of the clothing industry. Especially abundant were cotton frocks in gingham checks, cheery solids, bright calicos, and vivid plaids or stripes. All had fitted bodices with belted waists and gathered or full skirts. Sweater sets and delicately detailed blouses remained popular throughout decade. Fads were huge—one of the most recognizable is the felt circle skirt with appliqué detail. (Think of the stereotype: ponytailed girl with saddle shoes, bobby socks, button cardigan, and poufy poodle skirt.) The wasp waist held the spotlight, and skirts tended to be either voluminously full or fitted and narrow. Such body-conscious styles precipitated the return of the corset and torso-taming girdles. Bras were engineered to push the bosom up and out, and the prominent or shelf bust is now associated with quintessential '50s style. Toward the end of the decade, designers began breaking away from the hourglass shape and showed some fairly architectural designs, especially in coats. The swing coat with its wide tentlike shape and three-quarter-length sleeves became a favorite.

By the 1960s a social storm was brewing, one that fractured fashion into a kaleidoscope of different styles. The postwar baby boom resulted in a large mid-'60s teenage population, and these young people soon spurred a revolution in fashion the likes of which had not been witnessed since the Roaring Twenties. The decade started quietly enough, with a slim new silhouette seen alongside the now-familiar hourglass shape. The full skirt and fitted bodice gave way to a straight shirtdress, and simple cotton shifts and slim flat-front pants were popular for the homemaker. Collarless and sleeveless dresses were preferred, with lean lines and undefined waist. They often came with a cropped boxy overbodice in matching fabric, a matching fabric coat, or both, particularly for special-occasion dresses. Solid pastel or neutral colors dominated the fashion palette.

No one designer "invented" the mini skirt, but British designer Mary Quant certainly made it popular by mid-decade. She and other Mod designers worked with bright colors and bold patterns, experimenting with materials like vinyl and metal while keeping to minimal silhouettes. Breasts and hips were not emphasized; rather, styles were reduced to a boxy or A-line shape. Several other style movements were afoot as well. Those that followed the folk scene were inspired by simple country wear like corduroy, flannel, and jean materials, which were cut into jumpers and skirts. Folk style eventually included bohemian elements mixed with second-hand vintage pieces. This trend evolved into the "hippie" look, which also embraced hip huggers and bell-bottom pants, long shawls, and head scarves tied bandeau style. Psychedelia burst on the scene in the latter part of the '60s and quickly became a dominant force.

Accessories

The three-quarter sleeve popular in the 1950s sparked the need for longer gloves, which were fashioned in all sorts of colors and materials, from durable leather to dainty crochet. The exposed wrist also cried out for bracelets (hence the term *bracelet sleeve*), which in turn called out for matching necklaces and earrings. Although these matching sets of costume jewelry, called *parures*, had been worn for decades, they reached their pinnacle of popularity in the '50s. Today they are highly sought on the vintage market, particularly if they're signed. Matching went a little overboard during the era: Shoes matched handbags that matched hats and matched gloves ... well, you get the idea. Sixties-era jewelry tended to be more minimal, but *huge*, and crafted in unusual materials. Plastic and metal were shaped into oversized earrings, pendants, and bangles. Pearls in short single or multiple strands were in vogue for the conservative crowd, who also preferred simple button-style earrings. Hippies, on the other hand, were known for their long strands of colorful beads, bangle bracelets, dangle earrings, and—let's not forget—the peace sign necklace.

Hats for the average woman tended to be small, but on the runways designers were showing dramatic portrait brims and lampshade styles worn by the fashionistas of the day. Embellishments on everyday styles were wide ranging, everything from flowers to feathers and veils. In the 1960s the pillbox style took hold as women sought to emulate America's First Lady, Jacqueline Kennedy, but innovative milliners created versions with oversized crowns and large brims as well. One of the most unique looks to come out of this time is the bubble toque. Over-the-top trims and details were common, with some hats completely smothered in a cacophony of silk flowers. Excess was in.

Shoes underwent a major style change during these two decades. At the beginning of the '50s high heels generally featured snub toes and thicker heels, but the sleek stiletto was gaining ground. It was adopted by the mainstream later in the decade, as was the pointed toe, but, as the years passed, the square toe and chunky heel took center stage. The '60s featured shoe fads galore—one fun one was the cropped, flat "space boot." Tennis shoes, ballet flats, oxfords, and loafers remained popular for casual footwear.

1970s through the 1990s

Before the 1970s most women generally wore dresses while out and about, but as the decade progressed trousers and pantsuits became increasingly the go-to outfit for the liberated gal on the run. The tailored blazer was a wardrobe staple, easily matched with pants or skirt. The dress silhouette changed from boxy to body conscious, and form-hugging jerseys or knits were the preferred fabrics. Dresses tended to fit close to the torso, with skirts that flared at the hem. Minis fell out of vogue by mid-decade, and hemlines dropped below the knee. Designers experimented with longer lengths, giving rise to the maxi dress, a gown-style dress that was casual despite its long length.

From the mid-1970s and into the '80s, the disco scene was in full swing. Glitter reigned supreme, seen in sparkly halter tops, satin bell-bottoms, and metallic platform shoes. Other trends included clingy jersey dresses with swirling hems, slinky jersey jumpsuits with wide legs and plunging necklines, and shaggy fur coats and marabou boas added drama. Hot pants made their debut at the beginning of the decade, coupled with tottering heels. The look was definitely sizzling.

New easy-care synthetic fabrics (polyester, nylon, and acrylic) were celebrated and ubiquitous, and they are still abundant in today's vintage market. In contrast, a burgeoning ecology movement created interest in all things natural. Consumers began looking at fiber content labels for cotton, linen, and silk in lieu of the synthetics that had become so popular. Lower price was starting to take precedent, so you begin to see a marked difference in quality. Small movements such as the punk or anti-fashion scene had their beginnings in the early 1970s, starting a trend in deconstructing clothing that continues today.

These fashion subcultures continued into the 1980s, with the result that this decade is probably the most eclectic so far fashion-wise. Everyone seemed obsessed with embellishment, from beading and appliqué to flounces, puffed sleeves, and voluminous skirts. The power suit for women was huge—literally. Proportions were exaggerated, especially those rapidly growing shoulder pads.

Early-1990s clothing is now firmly classed as vintage, and some styles are highly sought-after. The bustier look that Jean-Paul Gaultier created for Madonna, those strapless poufed-skirt mini dresses for prom, cute and sexy styles by Betsey Johnson, innovative designs by the likes of Thierry Mugler . . . these are looks we may remember from the first time around, but they are iconic of their time and the interest is there to wear them again.

Accessories

By the 1970s hats were no longer considered a wardrobe essential—they became more of an individual statement—and big '80s hair all but destroyed the already dwindling millinery market. Wide floppy brims are a signature look from this era,  and there was a revival of certain vintage styles like the wide-brimmed straw hats reminiscent of Edwardian days, the '20s cloche, and the veiled '40s look.

Platform shoes were all the rage in the early '70s, but the fad ended quickly. Over the second half of the decade, sexy strappy sandals with skinny heels dominated for evening. Knee-high boots with stacked heels were worn indoors and out. Envelope bags with long thin shoulder straps were also a common trend. Jewelry designs became less showy and more delicate in the '70s only to be blown up again to enormous size in the '80s, when gigantic neon earrings and beads became a signature statement.

THE TWENTIETH CENTURY WAS AN EXCITING time for fashion—each decade provides its own muse and inspiration. It is this eclectic medley of style that makes vintage such a rich market. But the vintage market is vast and still fairly untamed. For many of us, that is part of its charm. Still, it's a good idea to have a few solid guidelines and some working knowledge before you start shopping. In the next chapter, we'll investigate the clues hidden in clothing that will help you know exactly what you're dealing with.

A Visual Time Line of Fashion Silhouettes

1900 1910 1920 1930

1940 1950 1960 1970 1980

Chapter 4

The Dating Game

SHOPPING FOR VINTAGE CLOTHING WILL surely involve a few mistakes and, occasionally, some regrets. When I was first in the business, I passed over a 1930s Elsa Schiaparelli gown because it had a plastic zipper, not a metal one. For me, that's the one that got away (and I doubt I'll ever recover!). We all learn as we go, but you can take steps to minimize the blunders and capitalize on the bargains. To be a savvy shopper involves detective work—studying clues in a garment's construction that help you guess its era or that, in some cases, give away exactly when a piece was made. You've got to know what you're looking at, so you can spot the treasures and find the deals.

Dating Dilemmas

IF YOU BUY VINTAGE CLOTHING FROM a seasoned, reputable dealer, they will automatically date things for you. But with the popularity of vintage has come a crop of sellers who lack this level of expertise. And if you shop at flea markets or thrift stores, you're pretty much on your own. In this chapter you'll learn what dealers most commonly look at to determine an item's date and value.

Let's take a closer look at some unusual and telltale details in clothing from the past, with the aim of dating and authenticating garments. As you investigate, keep in mind the first rule of detective work: Consider all the evidence. Don't rely on just one piece of information. At times the clues may contradict one another, so approach each object with an open mind. Look at the garment's style first, and keep that uppermost in your mind, then tally up the other clues. Most of all, have fun!

Silhouette

One of the first clues to look for is a garment's overall outline, or *silhouette*. The visual timeline on page 65 shows the most common silhouettes for each decade. You'll probably notice that many resemble recent clothing styles. That's because designers have always looked to past fashions for inspiration, so it's difficult to rely on design alone to identify era. Dealers and knowledgeable shoppers use several criteria to determine an item's age. It's important to keep in mind that in this process there are few absolutes but many "most likelies." Practice makes perfect: The more vintage you see, the more accurate your assessments will become.

Tags

Tags are the first thing you should look at, though they may be hard to find. Sometimes they're obvious and may even be pinned to the garment in the form of paper tag (like those shown, *right*), which contain valuable information. Other times tags and labels are stitched into more hidden places, such as a seam or hem, behind the neck, under the lining, or on a facing. If you take the time to compare old tags to newer ones you'll begin to get a sense of their look and feel, even if you don't recognize the maker. Observe graphic elements and the script or lettering style: Tags generally reflect the prevailing aesthetics of their time. Again, the more examples you examine, the more quickly you'll spot the characteristics of each era. A designer's or manufacturer's name may help determine a piece's value, but it does not always pinpoint the creation date. The next chapter explains all the different types of manufacturer and designer labels you'll likely encounter.

Fortunately, other clues can come to your rescue. Today's garments must carry detailed identification tags—noting things like fabric, care, size, and country of fabrication—but that wasn't always so. If you see a tag with complete fabric identification, especially if it's broken down into percentages, chances are good that the garment dates later than 1960 (see

the example, *right*). The Textile Fiber Productions Identification Act, which went into effect March 3, 1960, stated that a garment must identify all fibers used in its construction, along with their percentages. Prior to that date, the manufacturer could choose whether to include such information, as either a label (fabric or paper) or a stamp. Laws in the 1940s mandated the labeling of wool products, the percentage used, and a notice whether the wool was reprocessed or reused. General fiber identification became more common in the 1950s, with the introduction and marketing of brand-name synthetics.

Another dating clue is the Woolmark symbol *(right)*. You may already be familiar with this industry trademark, which is still in use. Not to be confused with government regulatory labeling, these trademarks are awarded by the Woolmark Co. (formerly the Wool Bureau) to manufacturers who meet stringent standards, and they are considered a sign of quality. The first Pure Woolmark symbol appeared in 1964, followed in 1971 by the Woolblend mark (for fabrics having a minimum of 60% wool), and, finally, a Wool Blend logo in 1999 (for fabrics containing less than 50% wool). If you see one of these tags, you can confidently assume the item is not dated prior to the symbols' use.

Care instructions were a later requirement. On July 3, 1972, the U.S. Federal Trade Commission passed a regulation mandating that textile manufacturers include care instructions for their products. Before that date, sewn-in care labels are not common. Labels or tags had to provide proper care instruction, such as dry clean only, machine wash/tumble dry, no chlorine bleach, and so on. Earlier manufacturers did sometimes provide this information on hangtags, but these were removed and discarded once an item was worn. The occasional 1950s or '60s label might indicate the use of a cool iron or no bleach, but usually not much beyond that. If you come across a sewn-in tag or label that states full care instructions, the garment likely dates to 1972 or later.

Look for fabric tags and labels. They will help you date garments, sometimes to the year.

Tags that include the International Ladies' Garment Workers' Union name or its initials (ILGWU; see page 74) declare that a product is union made. Although rare before 1940, they can be found in much vintage wear, sewn into a seam or lining. Founded in 1900, the ILGWU merged with other unions over the years, and these changes were reflected in the tags. Because this information also indicates the period in which a garment was manufactured, the tags are helpful in narrowing down the age of an item. Another common union label is that of the ACWA, or Amalgamated Clothing Workers of America. These labels include copyright dates indicating the unions' inception, and since the clothing would have been made within a few years of this date, narrowing the time period is easy.

UNION LABEL TIMETABLE	
1900–36	ILGWU–AFL *(unlikely to see a label from this period)*
1936–38	ILGWU–CIO
1940–55	ILGWU–AFL
1955–95	ILGWU–AFL-CIO
1995–2004	UNITE

The National Recovery Act, in effect in the United States from 1933 to 1935, served to promote fair competition in business as well as fair labor. Some manufacturers had labels put into their products to indicate they were in compliance with these guidelines. If you see a tag with a stylized blue eagle and the initials NRA you can be assured the item dates between those years. This is true for clothing and accessories. Many hang tags and a few designer or store labels include addresses. Zip codes were not introduced in the United States until 1963, so if a zip code is included, the item dates after that.

Buttons

Closures are next on the list of clues to hunt down. Until the 1930s, garments were held in place with buttons, hooks and eyes, and snaps. Turn-of-the-century buttons were made from natural materials like mother of pearl, tortoiseshell, metal, bone, and glass. Buttons made from early forms of plastic (i.e., celluloid and Bakelite; see page 77 for testing tips) appeared in the 1920s but were most popular in the '30s and '40s. Many were large and had two-tone or carved designs. World War II restrictions resulted in fewer buttons per garment and a tremendous number of cloth-covered closures, which remained popular well into the 1950s. By that decade, cheaper plastics had been invented and could simulate natural materials. Since the 1950s, plastic buttons have been the most commonplace.

When examining an item, keep in mind that buttons could have been replaced at any time. It was a fairly common practice to update a garment's look by changing to more modern buttons, and you'll frequently encounter replacements on coats especially. Close examination will usually reveal old threads or sewing marks where the previous buttons were attached. Note that if the button replacement is obvious, it can diminish the garment's value, especially if it is a designer piece.

Zippers

Zippers are an old standby for dating vintage. The zipper was invented in the late 1800s as a shoe closure, and by the early 1930s they were being used in handbags, corsets, outerwear, and sportswear and children's wear. These early metal types were bulky and ill suited for use in dresses. In the 1930s smaller zipper closures became available, but it was not until the end of the decade that they became widely used in dressmaking. Most often a '30s era dress closes on the left with snaps stitched into the side seam. Delicate brass zippers can be found at the back of the neck and even at the wrist on some 1930s–1940s dresses, along with some sort of side closure. Pre-1960s zippers nearly all have teeth made from metal, with rare exception. Elsa Schiaparelli and a couple other designers did experiment with plastic zippers all the way back in the late 1930s, but pre-1960s garments with plastic zippers are extremely rare. Brass zippers tend to date before World War II, and aluminum or steel after that.

Although plastic became the material of choice beginning in the 1960s, metal was still used, especially by home sewers and dressmakers. Clothing made in other countries, notably Mexico, often had metal zippers. By the 1970s most ready-to-wear garments had plastic zippers, although metal was usually used for outerwear and trousers

When vintage shopping, always look to see if the zipper is original. Since zippers are prone to breaking, keep in mind that some vintage you come across might have later replacements. If you are suspicious, look for signs like a different thread color or old stitching lines. Any replacing will affect value, so you could get a bargain. I have a beautiful beaded velvet gown from the 1940s that I picked up for a song at an estate sale because someone had replaced the original zipper with a plastic one. The collectors' value was diminished, but I got a lovely wearable piece of vintage for a very good price.

General Construction

How a garment is made can also offer a few clues to its vintage. Later, in the "Labels & Pricing" chapter, we'll talk more about construction as it relates to quality and value in the vintage market, but here are a few of the most important details to look for when trying to determine age.

Seams

First, I look at the seam finishes. Prior to the late 1960s, most off-the-rack clothing had seams that were "clean" finished, meaning that the edges were left raw and pressed open. To prevent fraying, some seams were sewn with a line of stitching near the edge, but most often the edges were "pinked." Pinking leaves a zigzag edge that resists fray. By the mid-1960s

Testing for Bakelite and Celluloid

Buttons and other decorations on vintage clothing are often made of these two early plastics. It's useful to be able to identify each of them.

Two Bakelite-testing methods I use are:

1. **The Formula-409 test.** If I'm at home, I soak a cotton-tipped swab with Formula-409 and rub it on the underside (or little-seen portion) of the piece, being careful not to get any on the fabric. If the piece is Bakelite, the cotton tip will turn yellow. Always make sure the surface is clean where you wipe and be sure to thoroughly remove the chemical's residue. Unfortunately, this test does not always work on black Bakelite.

2. **The rub test.** If I'm out in the field, I rub the surface briskly with my thumb until the material feels warm. I then sniff the piece immediately—Bakelite will have a scent similar to formaldehyde. The smell will be faint, so avoid wearing heavy perfumes on Bakelite-testing expeditions!

To test for celluloid, first I feel the weight of the button. Celluloid is very light, and not very strong; many pieces show cracking. If possible, I try the rub test, looking for a slight camphor smell. (This test may be impossible if the piece is fragile.)

If plastic buttons are neither Bakelite nor celluloid, they probably date after the 1940s, when cheaper plastics came into heavy use.

more manufacturers began overlocking seams. The overlock machine (also called a serger) binds together both edges of a seam with a series of "locked loop" threads. This method joins the seam, finishes the edge, and trims the excess fabric, all in one step. Merrowed edges are a type of overlock, but the seam is more narrow, just ¼ inch or so. The Merrow machine was invented in the 1800s, but before the 1960s its use in clothing was mainly confined to knitwear and swimwear, rarely on woven materials. Overlock seams on a woven garment generally indicate that the item was made in the 1960s or later.

On high-end, better dressmaker, or couture vintage you might see any number of seam treatments. Some have hand-cast finishes, folded or silk bound edgings, or French seams, which fully enclose the raw edge. Sadly, handwork of any kind is rare in more contemporary clothing unless it is couture, but older fashions often reflect time-consuming touches, even on everyday clothes. Fabric-bound buttonholes with hand finishing can be found on most vintage coats and suits, even those that were modestly priced for their era. Look closely at linings to see if they are set in by hand or if decorative work is hand done. As the decades progress, you see less and less of these labor-intensive techniques used on anything but the most expensive garments.

Linings

The use of linings has also changed over the years. In general, few dresses that date prior to the 1980s have full linings; some dresses from the 1920s and early '30s came with matching underslips, but since then slips have generally been purchased separately. Through the 1960s proper dress included the wearing of a slip, making a full lining redundant. Skirts sometimes had attached underslips, though. In the 1970s fashions were more body conscious, and some women chose not to wear slips. Dresses were seldom lined, though the practice of providing a separate matching underslip was resurrected. In the 1980s you begin to see full linings as women began to abandon slips almost altogether. So if you see a garment with pressed-open, clean-finished seams and no full lining, it is very likely vintage. Women's tailored suit jackets, on the other hand, were almost always fully lined. In the 1970s you see some jackets emerging with partial linings similar to those in men's blazers, but rarely were such shortcuts taken before that decade, except on the cheapest garments.

The bias cut was heavily favored in the 1930s for all kinds of dresses and lingerie. It fell out of favor during the years of World War II because of yardage restrictions. Bias-cut lingerie, however, did remain popular until the end of the 1940s. There was renewed interest in the use of bias in the 1970s, and it has continued to be a trend off and on since then.

Fabrics

Fabric is another good indicator of age. Cottons, woolens, and silks have been used for centuries to make clothing, so in your vintage shopping adventures you will certainly come across items made from these natural fibers. Beginning in the 1900s, textile innovations allowed for a wider range of manufactured and synthetic fibers. Different types of fabric were invented or introduced in specific years, so knowing the fabric will give you a pretty good idea at least how old it is.

Unfortunately, due to the lack of content tags, you may not always know exactly what type of fabric the item is made of. The good news is that there are easy tests you can do yourself to determine fabric content; these are detailed on pages 136–137. Knowing the fabric type is also useful for helping you determine how to clean and care for your garments.

Here are a few of the major synthetic fabrics and the dates they appeared on the market.

Manufactured Fibers Time Line	
Acetate	1920s on; more popular from 1940 on
Nylon	nylon stockings in 1939, other apparel beginning in mid-1940s; Qiana developed 1968, popular in 1970s
Polyester	Dacron polyester introduced in 1950; polyester used prominently after 1958
Rayon	1920s on; very popular in the 1940s
Spandex	Most common brand name is Lycra; developed in 1958

Rayon & Acetate Fabric made from Viscose (a wood-pulp material) was called artificial silk in the early 1900s and did not become known as rayon until 1924. Acetate, another cellulose-based synthetic fiber, was produced for commercial use in the 1920s. Early rayons and acetates were not well received because they were weak, especially when exposed to water. During the Depression their low cost made them more desirable, although cottons and silks were still preferred. In 1940 a major breakthrough made rayon fibers much stronger. This innovation, coupled with wartime restrictions on other fabrics, made its popularity soar. A great deal of 1940s vintage is made from rayon, which comes in nicely colorfast solids as well as pretty prints and patterns.

Nylon First used for stockings beginning in 1939, nylon was soon being made into other types of apparel as well. A few designers experimented with it in the 1940s, and in the 1950s it was used occasionally for dresses and often for lingerie, but nylon didn't become a truly popular dress fabric until the 1960s. In 1968 the DuPont Company created Qiana nylon, which had a wonderful drape and luster that many thought rivaled silk. Qiana was extremely popular throughout the '70s.

Polyester & Acrylics Polyesters, including Dacron, soon became widely used beginning in the 1950s, along with acrylics such as Orlon. Other trade names you might see on hangtags or labels include Celanese, Kodel, and Vycron (polyesters) and Acrilan, Zefran, and Creslan (acrylics).

Spandex In 1958 Lycra, a new elastic fiber, was introduced by the DuPont Company. Other companies quickly followed with their own versions of "spandex." The material found its greatest use in the swimwear and exercise-wear markets, and now it's incorporated for stretch into all types of garments.

EVEN IF YOUR ATTRACTION TO VINTAGE is purely as wearable fashion, knowing how to identify era will help you make better value choices. It will also aid you in knowing how to properly care for the purchases you do make. In this chapter, we provided you with some basic clues for dating vintage, but there are also excellent online resources to help you. Many vintage-clothing web sites have information pages devoted to tips and tricks for identifying dates of manufacture, and the Vintage Fashion Guild has a question-and-answer forum so that you can ask the experts. But there is nothing like personal experience to help you develop a "sense" for the age of clothing. It helps if you can see pieces in person, to feel the fabric and examine the details. To do so, I suggest attending some of the larger textile and vintage shows, where many highly reputable dealers ply their wares and await your perusal.

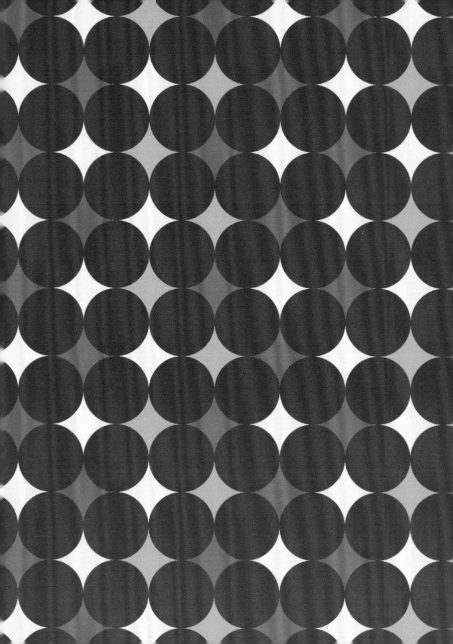

Chapter 5

Sizing It Up

WHETHER YOU'RE NEW TO VINTAGE or a seasoned collector, the sizing of vintage clothing can be confusing and just a wee bit frustrating. Why does a dress that says it's a size 12 look like something only a runway model could squeeze into? Mostly the reason is that styles have evolved dramatically over the past century, and sizing standards have changed along with them. Though it's true that the cut and fit of yesteryear's clothing are quite different from those of today, don't be discouraged. With a little knowledge and a few guidelines, you'll be able to choose clothing that's just your size and well suited to your body type.

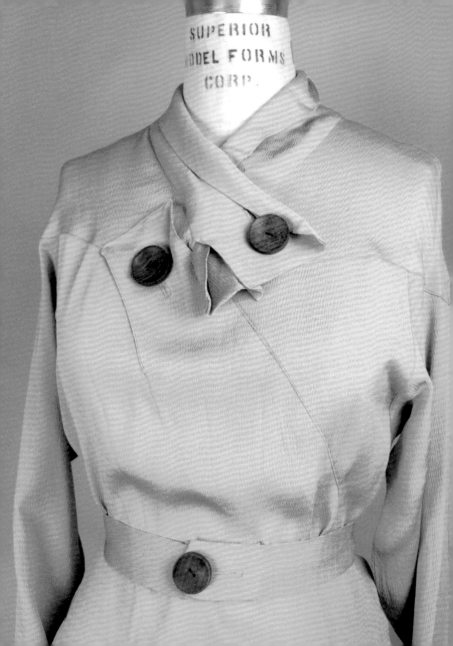

What Size Is It?

THIS IS THE MOST FREQUENT QUESTION that my customers ask. Most are puzzled when I explain that in the vintage trade we generally disregard size and concentrate instead on *measurements*. They want to know why. Over the past century, the apparel industry has attempted to set standards for sizing, but guidelines were never mandatory. And since it has always been easier to sell a garment with a smaller size tag, their efforts have had little effect. These changes account for approximately one full size every decade. No wonder that size 12 vintage dress is so tiny!

Most vintage clothing is much smaller than what the size on the tag implies. That's because the garment industry is constantly reinventing clothing sizes to reflect and appeal to consumers. For example, in the 1940s a typical pattern for a U.S. dress size 12 had a 30-inch bust, 25-inch waist, and 33-inch hip. That's not even a size 4 today! Another factor that determines fit is proportion. The silhouettes and styles from each decade have their own signature proportions. High or low waistlines, tight arm holes and short sleeve lengths—these are just a few of the design characteristics you'll encounter. Those who are new to vintage often mistake these fitting quirks for flaws, but really they're not. It's important to know the difference between a poor fit and an unfamiliar cut.

And speaking of cut, thanks to the casual styles of the past few decades, most of us are used to looser, generously fitting clothing. If you live in stretchy fabrics, you may be put off at first by the exacting cuts of vintage. What was once considered a proper fit may now be perceived as constricting movement. A lot of customers comment on how snug the sleeves feel on a vintage dress, particularly those from the 1950s, '60s, and even the '70s. You may also find that the waistline is small in proportion to the rest of the garment. Well, the secret's out: Until as recently as the '60s, women wore pretty complicated undergarments designed to mold the body to fit each era's ideal silhouette. Bras lifted and shaped the bustline; waist-cinching girdles and corsets tamed the midriff. Fortunately, if you have your heart set on a dress that's just a little snug, those original body-shapers are still plentiful throughout the vintage market, often in unworn and wearable condition.

(And they seem to have made a comeback, so you can now opt for contemporary versions of the good old girdle.)

Another problem area you may encounter is the shoulders and arms. Today's garments are roomier than those of yesteryear, when the style favored snug-fitting clothing. To show women that it's still possible to comfortably wear these closely cut dresses and blouses, when they try them on I ask them to straighten their shoulders and stand up straight. They're usually amazed by how a simple change in posture can cause a garment to fit better! The shoulders no longer feel snug and the chest fills out nicely. You may have seen movies in which young ladies were made to walk with a book balanced on the head. Chin up! Shoulders back! Chest out! It'll do wonders for you.

The Right Size for You

Step one in buying vintage is learning how to determine a good fit. First, you must record your body measurements. To do so, you'll need a good-quality cloth (not paper) tape measure, available in any fabric or craft store. You can measure over lightweight clothing or underwear. Refer to the illustrated-figure chart on the next page and measure each section as pictured. If you are uncomfortable doing this task on your own, make an appointment with a local dressmaker or tailor who can do it for you. (They may charge a small fee.) When measuring yourself, hold the tape loosely, except when determining the waist, where you should pull a little more closely (but not too snug). The chart indicates those measurements you should keep on hand when purchasing any type of vintage clothing. Some you will hardly ever use; others will be indispensable. But record them all.

Another option is to use a garment that fits you well and take its measurements according to the chart. Common sense says to check your measurements if you gain or lose weight, but you should update them once a year regardless, since bodies change subtly over time.

If your proportions are considered "average," congratulations! You should have an easy time navigating fit armed with just these basic measurements. But most of us do not fall into the "standard proportion range." You're probably already aware of your own personal fitting issues from past clothes-buying experiences. Broad or narrow shoulders, high or low waistline, long limbs . . . the list of unique features goes on and on. Here is where you will

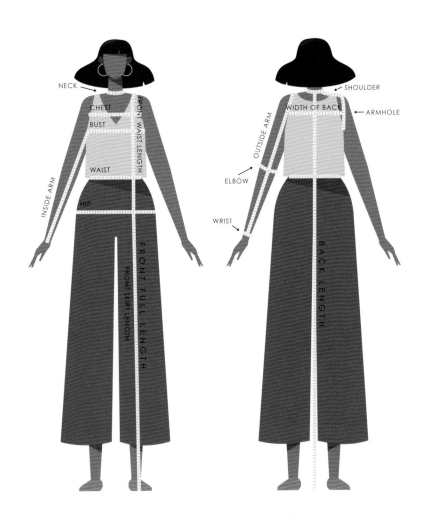

want to ask the dealer for more detailed measurement of the garment you're considering. Tell them your fit concerns. For example, if you have a long torso, a dress may not fit you properly even if it has your same waist circumference. That's because the *bodice length* (the measurement from the collar to the waistline) may be too short and will ride too high. If you explain this concern, most dealers will ask your neck-to-waist length. They can then measure the dress and see if it will work. Whatever your fitting issue, tell the dealer, and, with the aid of your chart numbers, they will be able to help. Here are some tips for measuring:

For comfort and to avoid straining fabric and seams, you will likely need to add to your actual numbers. This is called "allowing for ease." For older

Measurement	Tip
Bust	At the fullest part
Hip	At the fullest part
Front Waist Length	Shoulder to waist
Front Skirt Length	Waist to desired length
Front Full Length	Shoulder to floor
Neck	At the base of your neck
Shoulder	Neck to armhole line
Outside Arm	Shoulder to wrist (arm straight)
Inside Arm	Armhole to wrist (arm straight)
Elbow	Arm bent

or delicate vintage: Add 1 inch (2.5 cm) at the waist, at least 2 inches (5 cm) across the bust, and 3 inches (7.5 cm) to the hips. Allow for 2 inches in each armhole and 1 inch to upper-arm measurements. For sturdier garments, an extra 1½ inches (3.75 cm) at the bust and 2 inches at the hips (the rest as above) should work. Do not add ease to shoulder widths. For knits, the before-stretch numbers should be a bit less than your actual measurements.

Since vintage clothing spans nearly a century of changing styles, unfamiliar lines can be confused with poor fit. A good example is the 1950s penchant for a nipped waist and fitted bodice. Today's designs seldom accent the natural waistline; they are cut either higher (a cut known as empire) or lower, and bodices are seldom fitted. If you're new to vintage, the signature 1950s waist might feel too high, and the bodice tighter than you're used to. As long as there is room to move and the material is not straining, you should be fine. I tell customers trying on items from any era to lift their arms as if dancing and to try sitting in a vintage dress. You should be able to do both with reasonable comfort. Good posture may sound like an old-fashioned concept, but it really does wonders for feeling more comfortable in vintage clothing. Plus you'll look chic and graceful, too!

The list that follows breaks down the main eras for which you can find the most wearable vintage clothing and highlights how the designs were intended to fit the body. It will help you recognize the differences between design versus fitting issues. Obviously, different figures lend themselves better to certain silhouettes, so don't be discouraged if the 1930s bias cut is not for you—you may find that the 1960s shift is the most flattering fit. Work with your best assets, and allow the clothes to highlight your charms.

1920s Expect dropped, undefined waists and flat bosoms (lack of darts or shaping). If the fabric pulls across the bust, the fit is improper; a smooth look is what you're going for. Sleeves are often very fitted, as are armholes and neck openings. Fitted is fine; tight is not. A neckline is too tight if you cannot easily slip in two fingers. You should be able to comfortably cross your arms in front or raise your hands over your head. Sleeves should not bind when you bend your elbow; if they do, they will likely tear from the stress.

1930s Expect bias-cut clothing that molds closely to the body and hugs the hips. It can be hard to tell if a bias-cut dress is too small, but go with your instincts and the overall appearance. The fabric should skim your curves and follow your figure but not look like a second skin; if the garment bunches anywhere, it's not a good fit. Sleeves may be narrow and armholes fitted, so move naturally to ensure they do not bind or rip. Bustlines tend to be low and waistlines may fall slightly below the natural waist. The late 1930s saw wider shoulder lines, foreshadowing the next decade's fashions.

1940s Wartime restrictions dictated shorter skirts, hitting just below the knee and sitting on the natural waist. Broad shoulders came into vogue as well; if the shoulder line sits comfortably and does not feel slouchy, it is a proper fit. Slacks sit high on the waist, almost above the natural waistline, and often have front pleats. The look should be smooth, with pleats lying flat, not wrinkling below the back waistband. Blouse cuffs and necklines are often fitted; you should be able to comfortably fit two fingers into the neckband and one into a buttoned cuff. Blouses and sweaters are short to the waist. Jackets and coats have full sleeve lengths, but three-quarter sleeves are sometimes seen in dresses and tops. The late '40s saw longer skirts (sometimes nearly to the ankle) and narrower bodices. Although fitted, a bodice should not gape in front or bind across the chest.

1950s Expect waistlines to be snug, but not too tight. Three-quarter or "bracelet" sleeves on coats, suit jackets, and dresses were stylish, showing off long gloves and wide bracelets. This look takes a little getting used to since modern sleeves tend to be cut overly long; a long-sleeved sweater or a pair of long gloves worn with a coat will pull the look together. Although the full skirt was popular, so were narrow "pencil" skirts, with just a vent or slit to allow ease of movement. You'll know that a fitted skirt is too tight when it curves in under the derriere or shows pulling across the hips or abdomen. Tops were often cropped at the waist, and if they rise above the waistline, they're too short for you. The exceptions are bolero-style jackets and "shrug" sweaters. Pants tend to be cropped and fitted, with high waists and flat fronts. Pants are too tight if they pull in the crotch or the fabric strains when you sit. The market offers a lot of 1950s junior wear (clothing made for younger women), especially the ever-popular strapless tulle or taffeta prom dress. These pieces tend to have high bustlines and a smaller ribcage.

1960s The decade's best-known fashion trend is the mini skirt hitting at, or just above, the knee. Even coats can be quite short. Shorter sleeve lengths are common in all manner of clothing—dresses, sweaters, blouses, jackets, and coats. As with 1950s clothing, these uncommon lengths are part of the charm. The waist line is less fitted. Empire waistlines and baby-doll looks were also popular and are commonly available.

1970s You can expect some clothing to be very "body conscious." Jersey and knits were popular and often close-fitting; plunging necklines were also common. Polyester shirts with their whimsical prints, a classic '70s vintage item, are usually cut really narrow in the body and sleeves. You know a shirt is too small if the buttons pull (or pop off!) and it causes gaping. Pants tend to be very high waisted, a style that came back into fashion in the late 2010s. Belts are smaller, made to fit the waist not the hips (where we tend to wear them today).

1980s You can't talk about this era's fashion without mentioning shoulders—*big* shoulders. It can be hard to determine a good fit on a tailored dress or jacket from the '80s. If the back area across the shoulder blades fits and the shoulder pads sit firmly, without slipping or moving around, the garment fits you fine. The "baggy" look was big, too. Tops and sweaters were slouchy and loose, often with dropped shoulders. Coats were roomy and almost reached the ankle. Pants were loose (but fitted at the waist). Consider an '80s garment to be too big if it is unflattering or overwhelms you (which it will easily do if you are petite).

Buying by the Numbers

Now that you know your measurements, how do you use them? If shopping online, you'll notice that most dealers list a series of measurements. Some are more thorough than others, but the basics usually include bust or chest, waist, and hips. Compare those numbers to the ones on your own chart. Keep in mind that the measurements that dealers provide are the *actual* ones taken from the garment—they do not allow for ease, or stretch. Do not buy anything that has measurements smaller than your numbers unless you intend to alter.

So, what can and can't be done to alter a garment? Most can be taken in fairly easily—within reason. Letting out is another issue altogether. A good dealer will be able to tell you a garment's alteration potential. Asking these questions will help you determine if changes are possible:

- Can it be let out or taken in safely? If so, how much?
- Is there a seam allowance? If so, will the old seam likely show?
- Is there a hem allowance, and will the old hemline show?

Altering the shoulders is a major job; I recommend against it unless you are very skilled at sewing or have a good tailor and believe it is worth the extra expense.

You can find some amazing treasures at outdoor flea markets, antiques fairs, and vintage clothing shows, so don't be afraid to visit them even though they likely lack dressing rooms. (They may have a makeshift changing area, however, so wear a bodysuit, leggings, or unrevealing undergarments as well as clothes that comfortably slip on and off.) Sales are usually final, so you definitely want to ensure a good fit. Bring along your tape measure and personal chart so that you can measure the garment and compare its numbers to yours. Lay it flat and pull the material taut when measuring. If the fabric is a knit, pull a little but don't stretch too much or your measurements will be distorted. Just double the numbers for circumferences. Length measurements are actual.

Hitting the vintage shops should be pretty stress-free since most have dressing rooms and helpful staff to ensure that you find the perfect fit. As always, communicate! Greet the owner and explain what you're hoping to find. You'll certainly walk out with something special, even if it's not what you were looking for.

In all your sleuthing and searching, I predict that one day you will almost certainly fall in love with a piece that just doesn't fit the way it should. Or maybe it's just too frumpy or old-fashioned, but you simply cannot pass it up. What to do? Try some creative repurposing! Chapter 9, "Altered States," offers ideas for turning ill-fitting or outmoded vintage into fun new wardrobe staples.

YOU NOW HAVE ALL THE TOOLS you need to navigate fit when shopping for vintage. The best tip is to be prepared. Record your personal measurements and keep them on hand; they are absolutely necessary when shopping online and at the flea market. Carry a sturdy tape measure when you go to fairs and antiques shows. Know your body and its proportions so that you can ask the right questions. Most dealers welcome inquiries; they know that a happy customer is a repeat customer. Finally, remember that each era has its own unique lines and silhouettes that affect the way the clothing fits and drapes. Some may feel different from what you're used to, but that doesn't mean it's wrong. Follow the guidelines, and you'll be able to easily and confidently purchase vintage clothing that fits well and looks stylish.

Expert Tip

Shopping for Plus-Size Vintage

MYA PRICE
OWNER AND OPERATOR,
MORE THAN YOUR AVERAGE (MTYA)
MORETHANYOURAVERAGE.COM

Outside of a very small size range, it can be hard to find quality vintage that fits. But don't give up on finding vintage clothes in your size.

Consider online resale platforms, swap events, and secondhand stores in your community, and keep an eye out for consignment shops that specialize in plus-size clothing (even if none are local to you, these stores may have online sales). Buying directly from other plus-size people, or from a seller who curates specifically for plus sizes, makes it more likely that you'll find something that fits. Give yourself time to go through a store thoroughly. If the racks are arranged by size, don't neglect the non-plus options—you never know what you will find on each rack, and some looser or drapier clothes in a smaller size may still work for you. Always try something on if you think there's even a chance it might fit, no matter the number on the tag!

Lastly, look for vintage pieces that will fit into your existing wardrobe, but never be afraid to step outside of your comfort zone.

Chapter 6

Labels & Pricing

HERE IS THE CHAPTER YOU'VE been waiting for: Pricing! Prices for vintage clothing can be quite confusing, and even dealers sometimes have trouble determining value. The key to savvy shopping is knowing when you're paying too much and when you're getting a deal. As in any secondary market, prices for vintage clothing are unpredictable and fluctuate with trends. Rarity, quality, and condition affect pricing, too, not to mention your source (flea market versus tony L.A. boutique, for example). A look at the hierarchy of labels unlocks a clue to the mystery and will be invaluable in your quest for vintage gold.

All About the Label

A LOT OF FASHIONISTAS WOULD RATHER travel ahead of the trends than follow them. They understand that if you shop outside of what's "in," you're likely to spot fabulous clothing for less. In vintage, even couture can sometimes be found at a manageable price if it's not on the latest "what's hot" list. I love all kinds of vintage, from no-name labels to haute couture, but my tendency is to be frugal when buying for myself. Vintage is perfect for breaking out of your comfort zone, expanding your purchasing power to include fabulous and affordable clothes you might never consider otherwise. I love custom-made 1950s and '60s dresses and suits from Hong Kong—they rival any couture work I have seen, and the fabrics are exquisite. I'm a sucker for pretty rayon dresses from the 1940s (and really don't care who made them). My closet is filled with inexpensive cotton blouses from the '50s and '60s that never seem to wear out.

Influential designers and couturiers who have shaped fashion are the celebrities of vintage. A beautiful piece becomes all the more special when you look inside and spy a much-coveted "important name label." And if the garment has the iconic look for which that designer is famous, it's pure bliss. Some names are common; others are more obscure. Depending on the item's rarity and desirability, labels can increase value—sometimes quite a lot. Yet most vintage you'll encounter on your shopping adventures will have a lower-profile label, or even none at all.

In my business, I divide vintage into five tiers of label "hierarchy," on which I base my pricing. Although this is my personal formula, most dealers have a similar method.

1. **Budget/brand name, ready-to-wear** Much of the vintage on today's market falls squarely in this category. It consists of off-the-rack clothing mass produced to follow the trends of the day, and it was sold at an economical price. Despite its more humble status, it is usually well made when compared to today's standards.

2. **Private dressmaker/homemade** Before the later part of the twentieth century, young women were trained in basic sewing skills. Women often sewed for themselves and their families. Some of the more fortunate families employed a favorite dressmaker or tailor. Generally this clothing carries no label, which tends to devalue it, so pricing often stays modest. If the piece is truly exceptional or dates from an early era, it can cost more. Pieces that have survived tend to be well made and nicely detailed.

3. **Better name and boutique** This genre is less plentiful. The fabric, quality, and design will be finer, sometimes with couture-level details and construction. Better-name labels came out of high-standard manufacturing houses with talented in-house designers, many of whom went on to become famous. For example, early on Geoffrey Beene designed clothing for a company called Harmay, and Bill Blass worked for the David Crystal company in the 1940s. Better name labels were sold in smart boutiques or fine department stores, and it was common for boutiques to add their label to the merchandise they sold. Pieces often

reflect important cutting-edge trends but lack the designer name. Price range is broad, from midlevel to high.

4. **Designer ready-to-wear** Aside from couture, this category gets the most attention and generally commands higher prices. It is less plentiful and the quality tends to be very fine. Some off-the-rack designer clothing is lower-end, but most falls into the higher price ranges. Value depends on the importance and popularity of the designer.

5. **Couture** The *crème de la crème*. True couture is extremely rare and highly prized. Couture fashion is akin to original artwork. Pricing is reflective of its uniqueness and high quality and can quickly soar to thousands of dollars.

Before recent times, it could take years of working in vintage to acquire a basic knowledge of the huge variety of labels used by designers, manufacturers, and stores. Thankfully, there is now an online resource provided by the Vintage Fashion Guild, a group of dealers dedicated to promoting the highest level of standards in the vintage market. Visit their site (vintagefashionguild .com) to view their catalogue of hundreds of pictures of vintage labels, with more added daily. Most are accompanied by a brief history and date. All are fascinating to look at and read about, providing a mini-lesson in fashions of the past.

So, as you can see, labels are vital when shopping for vintage. They provide myriad information and are often just plain fun to look at. On most better garments they will be tacked in by hand, though stitching is extremely common. Now let's take a look at how they affect value so that you can make wise and informed purchases.

Price Guides

How much should you expect to pay? The answer is tricky. Like all fashion, vintage is affected by availability and popular demand, and prices are constantly rising and falling along with the latest trends. When determining prices, dealers must also consider aesthetic appeal, so even lower-end budget-label clothes will cost more if a piece is exceptional visually. In the retail price guide on the opposite page, I've tried to provide a sliding "yardstick" for budget and better-name vintage in good, clean, wearable condition. (Designer and couture vintage are not included due to the unpredictability of the prices, which are generally high.) The list focuses on midcentury vintage and later; anything that dates prior to the 1950s will probably cost more due to scarcity, and prices increase as the merchandise gets older.

Let's explore the hierarchy more closely, including some identification tips that will help with your appraisals.

Budget Wear

Due to its abundance in the marketplace, budget wear is the least expensive category. Like today's low-cost brands, yesteryear's manufacturers made clothes that were easy on the pocketbook—then and now. For decades, mail-order catalogues and low-end department stores offered less-expensive choices to a mass market. The budget ready-to-wear market has always been vigilant about spotting the next fashion shift and is quite adept at mass producing the "look du jour" at a reasonable price.

Affordability is a great plus of low-end vintage. Still, it helps to know how to recognize what's low-end so you don't overpay. By today's standards, clothing in this category is generally well made. Manufacturers worked

Retail Price Guide

Category	Budget Wear Private Dressmaker & Homemade	Better Name & Boutique
Coats	$40–$100	$100–$350
Day Dresses	$25–$85	$75–$150
Special-Occasion Dresses	$35–$200	$75–$350
Separates (sweaters, blouses, skirts)	$15–$50	$50–$150 (may be higher for cashmere or beaded)
Lingerie (includes brassieres, foundation garments, slips, peignoir sets, nighties, and the like)	$8–$45	$45–$100 (may be higher for silk or extra fancy examples)
Shoes	$25–$75	$45–$175
Handbags	$10–$50	$50–$250 (luxury leathers may go much higher; e.g., crocodile/alligator, ostrich, exotic skins, etc.)
Hats	$15–$40	$35–$125

NOTE: Prices can go higher or lower, but this is a general range.

hard to create a good-looking product at a lower price, and designs can be surprisingly attractive. The major difference lies in quality. Companies saved money wherever they could, so construction was simple, with little finish work and almost no hand stitching. Seams and hem allowances were modest (and sometimes downright skimpy). Buttons and trims were cheap. Fabrics tended to be flimsier, and linings or facings were minimal.

There are lots of different economy labels. Some sport a company name, such as Gingham Girl, which produced wonderful cotton day dresses in the 1950s, or Ship 'n' Shore, which has been manufacturing economical blouses since the mid-1950s. National department store brands such as Sears and JCPenney have long been adept at mimicking fashion trends—I find a lot of wonderful 1960s and '70s Mod vintage clothing with Sears labels. Some budget vintage will have no maker's label at all, probably because the firms sometimes used paper hang-tags, which were removed after the item was bought and worn. But garments generally have other types of tags, including union labels and fiber content or care instructions (see chapter 4, "The Dating Game," for more on these types of tags). When a maker's label is present, a name that's printed instead of woven is usually a good clue that you're dealing with budget wear.

After the 1960s, important designers began producing their own ready-to-wear lines, including Pierre Cardin and Halston, who licensed their names to low-end manufacturers. Yet even if budget wear has a designer name, it generally has less value. Two noteworthy exceptions are Mary Quant, who was such an important trendsetter that even her JCPenney line is highly prized, and Halston gowns (a Halston IV gown seldom sells for less than $200). In general, though, I would not pay much more for a designer budget-label piece than I would for a "no-name" garment.

Private Dressmaker & Homemade

Our second category is devoted to vintage without labels or tags, either because it was home-crafted or privately made by a dressmaker or tailor. The market tends to overlook "dressmaker" vintage, and it is commonly viewed as less desirable. That's unfortunate because many home seamstresses and independent dressmakers/tailors were highly skilled and produced perfectly lovely garments.

Pieces in this category usually lack any type of identification. Check all the seams to see if there is any type of union tag or size, care, or fabric-identification label. Occasionally, the makers ordered custom labels from ads in home magazines. These labels, most commonly found in hand-knit sweaters, generally say something like "Made for You by," with the person's name printed below. Sometimes fine fabrics were sold with a label and even a signature lining. The Pendleton wool company made garments and also sold yardage of their beautiful wools, with a label included. Also, Vogue patterns sometimes came with labels that could be sewn into a finished garment.

Construction offers more clues to identifying this category. One-of-a-kind hand-done pieces invariably give themselves away with slight irregularities in stitching or construction. Check seam edges as well as facings and hems for signs of hand cutting. Examine closures closely: Is the zipper perfectly aligned with the seam? Are buttonholes even? Manufactured garments have a uniform look, the result of having been mass produced on assembly lines. Finely tailored pieces can be more challenging to detect, especially if a lining prevents you from inspecting the interior construction. Custom-made clothing on the couture level is even trickier, though other clues give this category away (see page 115).

Homemade and dressmaker vintage is usually lower priced, but that doesn't mean it's inferior. If the garment is attractive and well made and you pay less than a comparable contemporary example, congratulate yourself on getting a bargain. Keep in mind that labels do fall out, so it's entirely possible (even for dealers) to mistake a valuable designer piece for something crafted by a better dressmaker. Keep your eyes open—you just might find a treasure for a song.

Better Name & Boutique

Not all couture has a famous designer name. If you're looking for a bargain, watch for undervalued creations by the custom shops of high-end department stores, smaller boutiques, and better manufacturers. This category makes up the mid- to higher range of vintage and includes a broad cross-section with more than one tier. Compared to budget wear, this type of vintage shows better quality and was usually (but not always) smarter in design. You can recognize these pieces by their superior workmanship and beautiful fabrics. They were more costly and exclusive in their day, and they still hold their value in ours.

Most major American and European cities had a handful of couture-level dressmaking houses. Before each new season, their wealthy clientele would visit the salons and place orders for garments created to their specifications. The construction and materials were exquisite, on par with those used by well-known designers. Today the names of these houses and their designers are mostly forgotten and examples are not so common, but if you do find them, the clothing is usually modestly priced and of high quality.

Within the context of this chapter, *boutique* refers either to small fashionable shops that carried exclusive, limited clothing lines or to specialty sections in department stores. Boutique pieces represented the most important trends and were beautifully designed and executed. They offer the same fashion-forward characteristics and interesting styles. Seldom do they command huge prices (unless they also carry a designer name), even if the merchandise may have been expensive in its day.

Many luxury department stores offered boutique venues, and several used the name "French Room" to denote more exclusive merchandise. Items might have been designed exclusively for that boutique or they might have been designer made. Many of the luxury department stores, like I. Magnin and Saks Fifth Avenue, commissioned designs to be manufactured under their own store label. A new type of boutique department blossomed in the 1960s when the youth of the day wanted their own signature fashions, separate from those of the older generation. One example of a boutique label is Biba, a shop opened in London in 1964 by Barbara Hulanicki and Stephen Fitz-Simon. They were on the cutting edge of the fashion revolution and carried hip, modern clothing that appealed to a young market. Because Biba clothes represent an important milestone in fashion history, prices can soar. Boutique clothing was always handpicked by savvy buyers or shop owners who had an excellent eye. It had to be special in one way or another: It might be on the cutting edge of fashion or terribly luxurious. Customers who shopped in these specialty sections wanted something unique and were willing to spend more to get it. If you are unconcerned with designer names but love great quality and design, this niche is perfect for you.

Not all better retailers were about the latest vogue. Shops like Peck and Peck, Abercrombie and Fitch, and Best & Co. carried well-made traditional clothing at a midlevel price point. In these labels is where you will find wonderful vintage wardrobe staples—pretty blouses and skirts, working day dresses, classic coats, impeccably tailored suits—that cost less than today's market. Again, this clothing is not cheap, but it usually offers good value for the dollar. Classic pieces tend to stay under the radar in vintage because they just don't carry the cachet of more iconic garments. A 1960s Peck and Peck skirt with perfect lines and lovely fabric would be something you can wear over and again, but its price would probably be less than delivery sushi for two.

A FEW DEPARTMENT-STORE BOUTIQUE LABELS TO LOOK FOR:

Playdeck	Bullocks Wilshire
French Room	Used by a number of better department stores
Young Dimensions	Saks Fifth Avenue
Brass Plum	Nordstrom
Miss Bergdorf	Bergdorf Goodman
The Trophy Room	Neiman Marcus (high-end designer)

There were also many brand-name manufacturers who distributed nationally to better department stores. They based their reputations on quality and incorporated the highest level of attention to detail, applying lovely dressmaker touches as often as possible. One fairly common vintage label that tends to be priced well is Suzy Perette, a company that, from the 1950s to the '70s, made special-occasion dresses whose designs were cleverly based on Paris originals. Another is Fred Perlberg, whose company created glamorous dance and party dresses. Pringle made lovely cashmere sweaters. Tailorbrooke and Handmacher were well known for exquisitely tailored suits. Vintage coats made from Harris tweed are still a handsome classic that wear well forever, and a vintage Cole bathing suit will always flatter the figure. Consumers back in the day were educated and demanding. If paying more, they wanted their clothing to wear well and last a long time. And fortunately for us, it has!

Designer Ready-to-Wear

With designer labels, vintage pricing begins to escalate, sometimes skyrocketing into the stratosphere. The more influential or iconic the designer, the more valuable their vintage clothing will be. In this section, we will talk about off-the-rack designer labels, also known as high-end ready-to-wear, or prêt-à-porter. The garments might have been limited runs, but they were not made to order, unlike couture. Couture, the highest level of designer wear, is never mass produced; each piece is custom made to order (see page 115 for more on couture).

Many great American designers manufactured their own ready-to-wear clothing, notably Hattie Carnegie in the 1940s. In her exclusive shop in New York City, Carnegie created couture on the second floor, but downstairs she sold ready-to-wear clothing and accessories. One of my favorite American designers is Claire McCardell. Her simple easy-to-wear, attractive, and original designs were sold exclusively off the rack, making them affordable to the middle class. McCardell revolutionized American sportswear, and her designs are scarce and highly sought today. Ceil Chapman, another name to remember, produced 1950s-era party dresses that are now wildly popular. In the 1960s, the Paris couturiers, struggling to compete with the ready-made market, began creating their own prêt-à-porter lines, and so did elite couturiers like Yves Saint Laurent, Valentino, and Chanel. At first they made limited runs and maintained extremely high standards (though later quality declined somewhat), so those early examples are well worth hunting for.

Pricing for designer vintage depends on many factors, but the designer name usually exerts the greatest impact. Also, styles that made a designer famous will invariably cost more than a generic piece. An original Diane von Furstenberg wrap dress from the 1970s can run $300, whereas another type of her dresses from the same era might be snapped up for as low as $50. Another important tool for helping to sort out value is quality, and it's often the easiest thing to assess. But if you're familiar with the labels themselves, you'll be much better off. They can be confusing, especially since designers use signature labels for each level of clothing produced in their house. Keep in mind that hundreds of designers and companies have helped to shape fashion history. Some you will recognize as still being in production today, such as Chanel, Dior, Valentino, and Calvin Klein. Others, like Fortuny and Vionnet, are so rare that most dealers go a lifetime without ever having one in their possession.

Of course, there are many books on designers and their histories, and the internet is a wonderful resource. Visit vintage sites and check completed online auctions to gauge which designer names are most highly valued at the moment. All dealers have their own biases and price accordingly. As you shop, let instinct guide you. If a garment's fabric, cut, and design are exquisite and the craftsmanship is superior, then a higher price is justified. Conversely, if the cost exceeds what you feel an item is worth and you are not totally smitten, then the answer is clear: Pass.

Couture

The highest echelon in vintage is the couture label. *Couture* is a shortened version of the French term *haute couture*. In my Nugent's French dictionary from 1952, *couture* is defined as "[to] seam or sew," and *haute* means "sublime, excellent, illustrious, haughty." In linguistic terms, then, *haute couture* refers to an exceptionally elevated form of sewing or dressmaking. It was first used during the second half of the nineteenth century to describe the work of Charles Fredrick Worth, a Paris-based designer with English roots who created custom-designed dresses for the cream of society, including the empress Eugénie. Since then the term has evolved to refer to one-of-a-kind, custom-ordered garments bearing the name of an extremely significant designer. The first recognized couturiers emerged in the early 1900s and included such paragons of style as Coco Chanel, Paul Poiret, Lanvin, Fortuny, Madeleine Vionnet, and Elsa Schiaparelli. All managed to elevate the craft of dressmaking to the level of art and profoundly impacted the course of fashion. Paris continued to produce celebrity couturiers like Balenciaga, Christian Dior, and Pierre Balmain in midcentury and, later, Yves Saint Laurent, Pierre Cardin, and Thierry Mugler.

In France, *haute couture* is a specific term as defined by the Chambre Syndicale de la Couture Parisienne. It is awarded to only a select few designers who meet strict requirements, one of which is that the designer maintains a workroom (*atelier*) in Paris with at least twenty full-time employees; only a tiny handful of exceptions have been made. The designer must also design, create, and custom-fit orders for clients, and, twice a year, the established houses must present a collection of 50 themed group runs to the press (newer houses are required to present only 35).

French rules for using the term *haute couture* have been accepted by the world of vintage, but *couture* has evolved into a broader definition. In vintage, a couture designer need not be Parisian, but his or her work must have been made to order. Garments must employ the highest level of craftsmanship and design. Couture is still an elite club, and few have been crowned with the title. Two of my favorite American couturiers are Adrian, who produced *the* most glamorous one-off gowns for Hollywood, and Sophie Gimbel, who offered custom-order designs at Saks Fifth Avenue for their Salon Moderne.

So how can labels help you pick out these rare gems? Since couture is one of a kind, the label may have a special-order number written by hand in pen somewhere on the side. The customer's name and a date may be found on a separate sewn-in label. Labels that read "adaptation," "adapted by," or "licensed copy" are another clue to watch for. In the early twentieth century, Paris couturiers battled against having their designs copied—patterns were taken from the originals to create garments that were then sold for much less. Some American firms were given a license to produce exact replicas in limited quantities. Although less valuable than the originals, and technically *not* couture, these pieces are still costly and historically important. Also, make sure the label does not say *prêt-à-porter*, which is French for "ready to wear"; less-experienced dealers sometimes confuse this with couture. If you purchase online, ask to see a photograph of the label. You should also ask if the dealer knows which year or collection the piece came from, or if they know the name of the previous owner. Chances are they don't, but it doesn't hurt to inquire. If you do buy a couture item and want to learn more about its history, you can try contacting the design house; they may research the

Expert Tip

Designer Dressing

R. LEIGH NICHOLLS
OWNER, THE COSMIC COWGIRL

Vintage couture provides an opportunity to own a piece of history and an affordable luxury. I concentrate on iconic pieces that represent a designer's body of work as well as revolutionary looks that define an era. I also collect classic items—like little black dresses and pencil skirts—that form the foundation of a unique yet timeless wardrobe.

Here are a few things to keep in mind when shopping for and collecting designer vintage.

- Research the designers you naturally gravitate toward. As you become more knowledgeable, you'll be able to refine your collection and develop specific areas of expertise.
- Learn about fabrics, cuts, findings, and couture sewing techniques. This will help you assess the quality of a garment and determine its authenticity. Things like sloppy stitching, puckered linings, and flimsy fabric may expose that a designer label has been added to a nondesigner garment by an unscrupulous previous owner.

- Condition is critical. Alterations greatly diminish value. Watch out for moth holes, fabric damage, and soiling. Ask yourself if you like the piece enough to have it repaired and if it is a significant enough piece to justify the cost of those repairs.
- Find an excellent cleaner who is experienced in the care of fine vintage clothing. If you live in a smaller town, you may need to send your items to be properly cleaned. Locate a member of Leading Cleaners Internationale (LCI), an organization of certified couture cleaners.
- Protect your collection. Preserve and maintain your valuable pieces by storing them in acid-free boxes and tissue. Make sure the storage area is climate controlled and not exposed to sunlight. Extreme temperatures and sunlight can easily destroy and fade fabrics.
- Finally, buy what you truly love. A great collection is assembled when you adore the pieces in it—no matter who designed them.

piece in their archives. Museum curators may also help you if you email pictures to them.

Like the couturiers themselves, couture clients have always been a small and exclusive group. If you're considering buying couture vintage, be cautious and research designers first. Surviving examples are rare, and prices are steep.

HOW MUCH SHOULD YOU PAY for vintage? There is no simple answer, what with so many factors affecting price, from demand and availability to condition and cachet. Here is my one word of advice: Know your threshold. Decide what you're willing to pay, and shop accordingly. Think in terms of what you feel is a reasonable price for a contemporary equivalent. For example, if your average price point for a pretty cotton skirt is $80, then you'll likely feel comfortable paying about the same for vintage. Don't be taken in by designer names unless the quality is there to match. If you do pay a high price, make sure there is good reason to do so. If you pause to apply the lessons learned in this chapter, you should be able to decide what to pay with confidence.

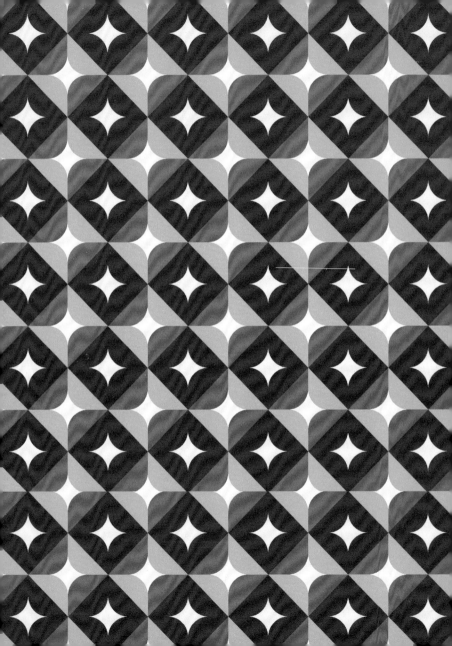

Chapter 7

Condition & Care

INCORPORATING VINTAGE INTO your wardrobe is a creative and intimate process. You will choose items that speak to your own special style. Much of what you collect will be one-of-a-kind, and many pieces you'll come to treasure. As contemporary styles change, your vintage will blend in with the new, lending a signature individuality to your look. Proper cleaning and storage will extend the life of your collection, plus good care offers an added benefit: If you're not one to become attached, you can later trade or sell well-cared-for vintage. Knowing what types of flaws to look for and avoid is vital, so in this chapter we'll point them out and reveal just when to mend and when to walk away.

Condition Report

LIKE A LOT OF DEALERS, I prefer to sell vintage that is in excellent or at least very good condition. There are occasions, however, when less-than-perfect vintage is too nice to pass over, especially when it's still perfectly wearable. And because flawed or soiled vintage sells for much less than "ready to wear" merchandise, you can score some great bargains—if, of course, you know what can and cannot be fixed.

Every vintage shopper has a different tolerance level for flaws and imperfections. I have had a few customers who inspect every inch of a

Detail of a stain that could make or break your purchase. Some are removable; many are not.

garment to make sure there is absolutely nothing amiss; they want the vintage they buy to look brand new. On the other hand are those shoppers who are more relaxed about minor defects and problems. If a dress they like has an inconspicuous spot, a bit of fade, or a little hole, they still consider it desirable, especially if the price is a bit lower. Only you know what you can bear. Just keep in mind that vintage has survived for years, decades even, and was probably used at some point. It's bound to show some wear and tear.

So, once you've asked yourself the obvious questions—Do I love it? Does it fit?—you'll definitely want to ask, What condition is it in? Condition is vital when buying vintage. It affects not only appearance but endurance as well. Dealers often use the term *vintage condition*, but what exactly does this mean? We all have our own method for describing "vintage" condition, with terms that help the shopper know what to expect. Mine is the following:

Mint	Never used, no visible flaws.
Excellent	Barely used, no visible flaws.
Very Good	Worn, but still in good shape. May have small flaws or repairs, which are explained. The repairs are not noticeable.
Good	Worn, but in good shape. Has small flaws or repairs, which are explained. On close inspection they are usually noticeable but don't really affect the appearance of the item when worn.
Fair	Items with noticeable flaws or repairs that are addressed. As a rule I avoid flawed merchandise, so most of these pieces have redeeming qualities, which I usually explain or comment on.

Before committing to purchase any vintage, examine it thoroughly. If you're in a shop or at the flea market, show, or similar venue, be sure to (1) look for stains or discoloration, (2) hold it up to a light to detect holes, (3) check the underarms, and (4) make sure buttons, collars, decorative trims, and the like are securely attached. If buying online, read the item description carefully and ask questions. Make sure you understand the return policy in case the item is not as described or does not meet your standards. Reputable dealers are very particular about flaws in their merchandise and conscientious about describing them to customers. You should be careful with online auctions such as eBay; check the seller's feedback. If you shop the flea market or thrift stores, all bets are off; it's unlikely you'll encounter a professional dealer, and items are generally sold as-is.

Some imperfections are easily repaired or simply not terribly noticeable; others should be avoided at all costs. Let's take a look at the most common ones so that you can easily distinguish the fixable faults from the fatal flaws.

Musty Dusty Spots & Smells

Not all the vintage you come across is going to be clean, fresh, and ready to wear. Stains and odors are two of the most common condition problems you'll encounter. Sometimes clothing was put away while clean, but years of storage have made it dusty and a bit musty smelling. Fortunately, these are not big problems. First try lightly brushing off and airing out the garment—that may be all it needs. If not, a regular cleaning should make a world of difference. (See page 138 for more on determining appropriate cleaning methods.) Slight mustiness can be eradicated, but a heavy mildew smell is tenacious unless the fabric it's infesting can handle strong detergents. Body odors are not always removable. You can try a special type of enzyme cleaner (such as Biz), but generally this is a flaw I suggest you avoid unless you pay next to nothing for the item and can afford to experiment. Unpleasant odors such as cigarettes and even mothballs can be removed with cleaning. To eliminate mothball smell, in addition to cleaning you will need to air out the item for a week or so, preferably outdoors (but out of the sun).

Old stains are another big issue—some may be removable, but many are not. They've often had years to set into the fabric and, in some cases, have deteriorated the fibers. Mildew is among the worst offenders; I strongly advise passing up clothing with obvious mildew stains. Removing any type of spot can be tricky at best, and since it's impossible to tell exactly what the spot is, you may have to try several methods. (See "Basic Spot Removal Step-by-Step," *opposite*.) Before using any type of cleaning solution, you should first test it in an inconspicuous place on the garment to make sure it doesn't react badly with the fabric. To do so, dip a cotton swab into the solution and press it to the edge of an inside seam. Look to see whether the dye runs onto the swab. After the solution dries, make sure it did not adversely affect the fabric. Look for fiber damage, discoloration, puckering, and dark rings. If the item cannot handle the cleaning solution, take it to a professional cleaner.

NOTE:

Do not try to remove spots from delicate or older vintage, especially silk, rayon, and acetate, which are easily damaged. And remember to feather out the area you're cleaning to prevent a ring from forming. Taffeta, satin, and faille are the most susceptible.

Basic Spot Removal Step-by-Step

For best results, try these steps, in order:

1. Start with plain warm water. Place an absorbent cloth under the stain and blot with a wet (but not dripping) cloth.

2. If water alone doesn't work (and it probably won't), try a little mild dish soap. A squirt or two in a medium-size bowl of warm water is enough. Rinse with a sponge and warm water.

3. If the spot continues to be stubborn, switch to diluted Biz laundry soap, which contains an enzyme cleaner. If the fabric is strong (i.e., sturdy cotton and linen or wool), you can wiggle the material very gently to break up the stain; don't overdo it. Rinse with a sponge and warm water.

4. Still there? Hit it with a squirt of Windex. (Make sure you do a test on the fabric first.) I have removed many a discouraging stain with this handy blue liquid.

5. Rinse out all solutions from the fabric with a sponge and let it air-dry.

If none of these methods work, you're likely stuck with a permanent mark, but there are still a couple tricks left. First, I try treating the area with a sponge moistened with alcohol. Next, I try a cleaning solvent like Afta. These can work on old grease-type stains. Formula-409 has also been known to remove stubborn spots, but I use it as a last resort because the chemical is harsh. Always remember to thoroughly rinse between each attempt and *be gentle*. Avoid rubbing; blot instead.

A few specific types of common stains are pretty easy to take care of, though keep in mind that you may never fully get rid of them. Set-in stains on white cotton and linen can be faded with some of the laundry whiteners on the market. Another option that works well is to apply a mixture of salt and lemon juice to the stain and set it out in the sun for a day. Diluted chlorine bleach also works but is extremely damaging to most fabrics, so I prefer OxiClean. For really bad spots, I have had great results by mixing a paste of OxiClean and liquid laundry soap and letting it sit on the area for a couple hours. Be careful, though, since the mixture may fade certain fabrics; be sure to test in an inconspicuous place first.

I consider rust stains to be permanent. They can sometimes be lightened with a paste of salt and vinegar, but all in all I suggest walking away from rust-stained clothing. Ink stains, however, are not as fatal as you might think. Plain old hairspray can remove many types of ink. Drip the hairspray right on the mark and blot; repeat until the mark fades, and then use a soapy solution. Remember to always rinse with plain water after using any type of cleaner. Lastly, clean the garment as appropriate.

There are many types of spot cleaners on the market, but I tend to stick to the basic ingredients mentioned above. Each vintage dealer has a preferred spot-removal method, but we all agree on one thing: Be as gentle as possible and stay away from damaging or harsh products. These include chlorine bleach, quick-soak cleaners, and strong detergents, which will likely damage the item beyond all hope.

Fabric Flaws & Sticky Zippers

The next type of condition problem you're likely to encounter is fabric damage. Some damages can be mended; others are permanent or, even worse, indicate further deterioration. One frequent problem is fading, which is usually found on the shoulders or down one or both sides of a garment. This phenomenon, known as *gas fading*, is permanent. Mild fading might not be noticeable when the garment is worn, but just remember that obvious fading is unable to be remedied. People sometimes overdye a piece to mask fading, but this doesn't always work well and can ruin the item. Only try it if you're willing to lose the garment.

The worst flaw in vintage is *shattering*, which is when fabric has deteriorated and is beginning to split. It is generally caused by one or more of the following: heavy metal dyes that were used long ago, the salt in perspiration, and atmospheric damage. There is no cure for shattering, and it will only get worse as the garment is handled. Shattering is very common on older silks (those from the 1920s/30s are notorious) and occurs most commonly across the shoulders and under the arms. It first appears as little slashes in the fabric; if you pull even gently, they will split even more. Very bad cases will cause the garment to literally fall to pieces. However, if shattering is contained to a specific area and the rest of the garment is strong, you can try piecing in a gusset of matching fabric. This procedure requires advanced sewing skills, so you may want to have a professional do it for you. You can take the fabric from a sash or inside pocket or even from the hem. (Note that you should not drastically alter historically significant or antique vintage.) I have sometimes reinforced isolated shattering from behind, using a piece of lightweight backing, though this technique is successful only if the damage is slight and the rest of the fabric is sturdy. But know beforehand: Ninety percent of the time, shattering is fatal.

Another form of fabric deterioration is dry rot, which is caused by storage in a hot, dry space. It can happen to any natural fiber and is also a fatal flaw. Any material that tears with gentle tugging should be passed over—it is beyond your help.

Older vintage garments were often sewn with all-cotton thread, which tends to weaken with age, so split seams are common. This fixable imperfection requires just a quick restitch. Simply re-sew along the original seam line, and all should be fine. Tears and holes are more problematic, and the mending can be quite noticeable. Close tiny holes or tears with a few little stitches in a matching thread color. A great trick for mending holes in lightweight fabrics is to split/unwind the thread and use a very thin strand; the mend will be less obvious. (You need to use good-quality twisted thread to get a strong enough strand.) For larger holes, weaving with a matching thread or applying a patch from behind are good—but still noticeable—solutions. Like gussets, patch material can be taken from an inside pocket or hem.

Next up in the condition review is moth damage, which is all too common in older wools and cashmere. Sometimes the damage does not go all the way through the material but looks like a shaved area. This is called *crazing*. With thick wools, you can make the area look better by raising the fabric's nap. Take a needle and gently pick at the area, lifting it with the tip. Do not tear or scratch at the material, just pick and lift. This will tease some of the fibers loose and re-create the fuzzy surface that was munched off by the moth. For holes that go all the way through, you will need to mend by reweaving with a matching yarn color. My trick is to tease out a strand of the garment's own fabric, either from the edge of a seam or a hem, and use that to mend.

(You may have to undo a portion of the lining to get to the raw seams, but it's well worth the extra work.) Mending moth holes is tedious, and if there are too many or they are large, I suggest you pass on the garment unless it is a real steal.

Knits and velvets are two other fabrics that often have special condition problems. Pulls in knits occur frequently and look awful. If the pull has caused a visible line in the fabric, you can sometimes stretch it out to be less noticeable. But be careful: On fine knits, doing so may cause a run. If it hasn't created a visible line, you can try gently pulling the loose thread to the wrong side of the garment, again being careful not to cause a run. My method is to thread a needle with a thin piece of fuzzy yarn, which, when pushed through the source of the pull, may catch the hanging thread and bring it to the back. If the pull has a long thread, I insert an empty needle into the source, thread the needle with the pulled strand, and slide it through to the wrong side. As for vintage velvets, they will sometimes have shiny areas where the pile has been crushed. Steaming and brushing can help raise the pile, but badly flattened velvet is permanent. If the affected area is obvious, like the derriere or the elbow, I pass, but a little under the arm will go unnoticed. Be sure to steam velvet from the wrong side or take it to a professional cleaner. Never iron!

The most benign closure problem is the "sticky" zipper that is difficult to slide up or down. All the remedy that's usually required is to lightly rub the zipper teeth with a bar of Ivory soap, which acts as a lubricant and will not hurt the cloth tape. Start by working a tiny bit of the soap under the slider— it doesn't take much—and when you've loosened it, rub a little soap over the teeth. Gently slide the zipper a few times; it should begin to work smoothly. (Make sure no fabric is caught in the teeth.) Do not force it or you might

break the teeth. You can do this trick on both metal and plastic zippers, though the latter tend not to stick as often. Broken zippers are a bit more serious. If the slider has popped off one side without damaging the teeth, you can try removing the metal stop bar at the bottom of the zipper and then carefully thread the slider back onto the zipper, making sure the teeth begin to lock. Then you must sew a strong bar tack in place of the stop bar so that the zipper does not separate from the bottom. Zippers with broken teeth or torn cloth tapes cannot be fixed and must be removed and replaced. A professional tailor or dressmaker can do this for you if your tailoring skills are not advanced.

Loose buttons are the easiest and most common mend—they simply require reinforcement with sturdy thread. Before wearing a newly purchased vintage item, check it over to ensure that the buttons are not loose or unraveling. Keep in mind, though, that buttons on outerwear are not supposed to be sewn tightly to the fabric. Without a thread shank, they will strain and pop off more easily. On coats and jackets, the button shank should be firm and wrapped without loose threads; the button will wiggle, but that's fine. Button holes can also become damaged over time. If the button hole is thread bound and the damage isn't too bad, you can reinforce the ends with a bar tack to halt the tearing. If the button hole is cloth bound, you can usually hand stitch the pieces back into place, as long as the corners are not torn badly.

Folks often pass on garments with missing buttons, but don't be too hasty to dismiss a garment you really like just because it needs a button replaced. First check the inside side seams—manufacturers sometimes attach spare buttons, especially on shirts, coats and blazers. No spares? Consider replacing all the buttons instead of trying to find a match. Etsy is my favorite source for finding vintage buttons. I swear you can find any type of button imaginable. Measure your original button and look for something with the same dimensions so it will fit through the buttonhole. It is quite likely you will find something similar to the original button, or you can go with something different just for fun.

A Note About Furs

Buying vintage fur can be tricky business. First are the legal issues. Many types come from animals now on the endangered species list, and even owning a vintage example may be illegal unless you have proof the fur was originally marketed before the animal was put on the list. Laws vary from state to state; for information, contact the U.S. Department of Fish and Wildlife. Fortunately, the most common types on the market—raccoon, mink, muskrat, Persian lamb—are legal, but it's still prudent to ask what type it is before you buy.

Next, furs can be quite deceptive when it comes to their condition. Unless properly stored, the skins can dry out and weaken. An old fur coat may look fine until you start wearing it, and then little splits might appear, most often across the shoulders and under the arms. This damage is difficult to repair. A few times I have been able to stitch the split together and I've had some success using rubber cement to laminate a piece of muslin to the back of the skin, but these repairs work only if the rest of the garment is in good condition. The best precaution is to examine a fur really well. A healthy fur will feel supple and smooth. Lift up the sleeves and check the underarms and across the back, rolling the skins to spot splitting. Check around pockets and under collars. Take a handful of fur and give a *gentle* tug—if a lot of hairs pull away, be wary. Don't worry about a few loose strands, though. All furs shed a bit, especially rabbit.

Once the fur is yours, treat it well. Never store it in extremes or under or in plastic. To remove dust and debris, brush the fur in the direction it lays. Wiping it with a damp cloth is fine (also in the proper direction), but never soak a fur to the skin. It can take exposure to rain or snow, but let it dry naturally, away from direct heat.

Tender Loving Care

ONCE YOU'VE PURCHASED A FABULOUS PIECE of vintage, how do you care for it and make it last? Today's clothing comes with tags of instructions, but vintage seldom does. Even fiber content can be a mystery. Fabric is the foundation of clothing, and knowing what type of material a garment is made from is important to determining how to clean and care for it. Seasoned dealers can usually identify the fabric and tell you how the piece should be cleaned. A novice dealer may not have this knowledge.

First, you should look for labels. If there are none, you may still be able to identify fibers using a burn test. (WARNING: Do this test very carefully, and never leave the flame unattended.) Procure a small bit of material from an inconspicuous place, such as an unfinished seam or pocket edge, or take a bit of fuzz from a sweater and roll it into a little ball. Secure the fibers in metal tweezers and hold them over (not in) a flame. Watch the reaction of the fibers before they burn, observe the burning, and then quickly sniff the smoke. Each fiber category has distinct characteristics when burned. If the material is a blend, the results will be mixed; pay close attention to smell in particular. Consult the chart on the next two pages to see what you're dealing with. It all happens in just a few seconds, so you might need to repeat the process to get the information you seek.

Fiber	Reaction to heat of flame before burning	Burning characteristics
Cotton	None	Burns quickly, no melting
Linen	None	Burns quickly, no melting
Rubber	Fuses away from flame	Burns rapidly, with melting
Silk	Fuses & curls away from flame	Burns slowly and tends to extinguish
Wool	Fuses & curls away from flame	Burns slowly and tends to extinguish
Acetate	Fuses away from flame	Burns, with melting
Acrylic	Fuses away from flame	Burns quickly, with melting
Nylon	Fuses & shrinks away from flame	Slow burn, with melting
Polyester	Fuses & shrinks away from flame	Burns slowly, with melting
Rayon	None	Burns VERY quickly
Lycra/Spandex	Fuses but does not shrink	Burns, with melting

Smells like	Residue after burning
Burning paper	Fluffy gray ash
Burning paper	Fluffy gray ash
Sulfur	Sticky mass
Burning hair	Round bead, black and brittle Note: Ash from weighted silk will hold original shape of fibers and glow red after burning
Burning hair	Brittle bubbly shape, crushes easily
Vinegar	Black, amorphous bead, brittle
Acrid	Hard, black, amorphous bead, brittle
Celery	Tan or gray bead, round and tough
Plastic/chemical	Black round bead, hard and tough
Wood or paper	Very little or no ash
Chemical	Soft, fluffy black ash

Cleaning Tips

Knowing a garment's material is important, but understanding its construction will tell you if it can be laundered or if it must be dry-cleaned. First on the list of items that need professional cleaning are most rayons and silks. If you try to hand-wash them, chances are great they'll be forever ruined. Every vintage dealer I know has at least one tragic story. For me, it was attempting to hand-wash a favorite 1940s rayon crepe dress. To my horror, my beautiful dress shriveled to child's size the second it hit the water. A tragedy, indeed.

Some vintage woolens can be hand-washed, but tailored items often have linings and facings that will likely shift and shrink. Even the gentlest hand-washing will irrevocably distort the shape. For the same reason, eveningwear and fancy dress should be professionally cleaned, especially if the fabrics are embellished. Note that old sequins may melt with dry cleaning; make sure your cleaner tests first. Water will tarnish beads and rhinestones and warp embroidery. Luxury fabrics such as tapestry and brocade should be professionally cleaned, and velvets absolutely *must* be. Leather, suede, and furs, both real and faux, must also go to a professional.

Always choose a reputable dry cleaner and ask if they are comfortable dealing with vintage. I have had some real disasters with inexperienced establishments. Cleaning can be expensive, but the good news is that tailored garments and eveningwear don't need treatment after every use. To limit the need for costly trips to your local professional launderer, try these common-sense tips.

Tip #1 **Perspiration protection.** Always use a clear, scent-free antiper-spirant when wearing important clothing and wait at least fifteen minutes after applying to get dressed. Perspiration and waxy deodorants don't cause immediate damage, but if left on fabric they will cause it to discolor and deteriorate. For close-fitting clothing, I suggest underarm shields. These crescent-shaped pieces of moisture-resistant material are tacked into a garment's underarms. They are still being made by a company called Kleinerts; you can find them in larger fabric stores or buy them online directly from the company.

Tip #2 **Brush and air.** Get in the habit of brushing your good clothing. Brushing will remove lint, tiny crumbs, and dust that can settle in and soil the fabric. Woolens and sturdy fabrics can handle a whisk broom, but for delicate material, use a softer garment brush and be gentle. Also, don't put your clothing into the closet immediately after wearing. Let it hang overnight to air out. You'll be surprised how fresh your wardrobe will stay if you get into this habit. Lastly, hang your woolens outside once a year. Wait for a dry, cool day with a little breeze and pick a shady spot to prevent sun fade.

Tip #3 **Spot cleanings.** It is not necessary to clean an entire garment when one or two new little spots pop up, but don't ignore them either. Even a spill that dries to look invisible will eventually discolor fabric and become a permanent stain. Remember to test all solutions in an inconspicuous place before undertaking spot removal. If in doubt, take the item to a professional cleaner soon, before the spot has a chance to set.

Hand & Machine Washing

Not all vintage needs to be professionally cleaned. Many articles can be hand washed, and some can even go in the washing machine, although I almost never use a dryer for my vintage. Hand-washable vintage includes simple cotton or linen dresses, skirts, and blouses; woolen sweaters (even cashmere); and knitwear that is unlined. Because vintage lingerie was made to be easily laundered at home, most is hand-washable, even silks and rayons.

You can hand wash one or two things at a time, but be careful not to mix light and dark colors. First, fill a large tub with warm (not hot) water and add a few squirts of gentle dishwashing soap. For cottons and linen, you can add a spoonful of your favorite nonchlorine whitener (I prefer OxiClean). Press down repeatedly to squish the sudsy water through the garment. Do *not* wring or twist. I allow the item to soak for an hour or so. To rinse, gently scoop out the garment in a bundle and drop it in a sink while you refill the tub with warm water. Return the garment to the tub and squish some more; repeat until all the soap is removed. Drop the garment back in the sink and push out as much water as you can, again *without* wringing or twisting. Lastly, lay a clean, dry towel on a flat surface, spread the garment on top, and roll the towel tightly to remove excess water. To dry sweaters, lay flat and reshape while wet, and then air dry. For smaller garments I use a folding wooden rack. I hang dresses, skirts, and blouses on plastic hangers. They wrinkle less that way.

Some vintage can handle being machine washed, especially the synthetics from the 1960s and later, which were developed with easy home care in mind. I often machine wash polyester or nylon dresses and blouses, but just to be safe I use the gentle cycle and warm water. I avoid the dryer, though; the hot air is harsh on fibers, and the tumbling pulls at seams. When it comes to your favorite vintage, just say no to dryers. You'll be happier, and so will your clothes.

Storage & Continued Care

Storing your vintage properly will help prolong its life, and the dos and don'ts are simple. First, get rid of any and all wire hangers in your closet. Return them to the dry cleaners, put them in the metal recycling bin, or make crafts out of them, but don't use them to hang your clothing. Metal hangers will irretrievably distort the shoulder lines and can also wear through fabric. In addition, they may rust, which leaves a permanent stain. Inexpensive, thick plastic hangers are fine, and if you want to spend the extra money, padded-cloth hangers work well and look nice. For coats, shaped hangers are best; they can bear the extra weight and will help preserve the shoulder shape. Skirts and slacks do best on clamp-type hangers—not the ones with pinch grips, which can cause marks. If you do use hangers with grips, make sure the grips are plastic or velvet lined, not metal, and put a piece of cloth underneath as a cushion. Velvets and wools are especially prone to damage from these types of clips.

Some articles of vintage should not be hung at all. Beaded dresses should be wrapped in acid-free tissue and stored flat in a drawer or cloth garment bag. The weight of the glass beads will compromise the delicate fabric. I recommend storing sheer delicate items as well as lace pieces the same way. Sweaters and loose knits should not be put on hangers, which stress and stretch the shoulders; fortunately, most knits can be reshaped when washed. Hats are best stored in boxes; the vintage market abounds with authentic examples.

Cellars and attics are notorious for destroying vintage clothing and accessories. Dampness causes mildew, and hot dry air will cause dry rot. For protection against mildew, not to mention nuisance wrinkles, never put away anything (especially outerwear) that is the least bit damp. Dry it in the open away from direct heat. Keeping the moths away from your wool, furs, and cashmere is another imperative. I often wonder how such a drab little creature can wreak so much havoc! If a moth can't find wool, it will attack silk or even food spills on fabric. The most important thing is to keep your vintage, as well as your drawers and closet floors, clean and fresh. Once a year, at least, vacuum all clothing storage spaces. Avoid moth balls; they are extremely toxic (especially to cats) and the smell is tenacious. Sachets of lavender and clove repel moths and smell nice, too. Cedar is an age-old moth repellent. You can find cedar blocks at any hardware store, and natural-food stores sometimes carry cedar oil to refresh faded blocks. If you buy any kind of secondhand woolens, brush them off (outside!), seal them in a plastic bag, and put them in the freezer for a few days. This destroys any moth larvae or eggs.

Pressing & Mending

Pressing your vintage should be done carefully. Use the appropriate heat for the fabric, and press from the back side whenever possible. If you must iron the front of the fabric, use a press cloth to prevent scotching and "shine." (A linen tea towel works well.) If you are lucky enough to own a good garment steamer, try to always steam

from the inside and keep the head moving so that you don't wet one area too much. Use spray starch on cotton and linen only if you plan to wear the item; for storage, skip the starch, which can yellow over time. To prevent creasing of sleeves, use a sleeve roll or roll up a thick towel and use that instead.

Check buttons periodically to make sure they are not coming loose—you would hate to lose an original vintage button. Verify whether snaps and hooks need reinforcing. You can ask your dry cleaner to do this for you. Mend small holes and tears immediately before they have a chance to grow any bigger. A stitch in time saves nine!

THERE ARE SOME GREAT BARGAINS to be found when vintage shopping, especially if you're flexible about condition. Flawed or soiled vintage sells for much less than merchandise that's spotless and ready to wear, so it's to your advantage to know how to carry out a few easy remedies. Yet when assessing condition, use your own good judgment. Balance the amount you're saving against the time and work required. I suggest trying any of the methods of cleaning and restoration described in this chapter only on the less expensive things you pick up at the flea market or thrift store. Experimentation is good, but it shouldn't be done on an item of value. There is something so satisfying in rescuing a wonderful piece of vintage. But be careful . . . You just might get hooked!

Expert Tip

Storing & Caring for Antique Garments & Textiles

KAREN AUGUSTA
OWNER, KAREN AUGUSTA AUCTIONS,
ANTIQUE LACE & FASHION
AUGUSTA-AUCTION.COM

The best way to store your antique garments and textiles will depend on their intended use. A collection of museum-quality pieces requires specialized storage materials and conditions; for an expert's guide, I recommend Margaret Ordonez's book *Your Vintage Keepsake*. If your antique clothing collection is for your wearing enjoyment and the textiles are intended for use in your home, a few simple precautions will help ensure that they will become family heirlooms enjoyed by future generations.

- Keep all fabrics out of direct sunlight for extended periods. Sun rapidly fades and breaks down fibers.
- Antique fabrics should never come into direct contact with wood and wood products, including cardboard boxes, dresser drawers, paper bags, trunks (even cedar), etc. The acid from wood products will leach into the garments causing all-over brown stains.

- Plastic storage is another no-no. All fabrics need to "breathe."
- Steaming for silks, wools, and synthetics is gentler than ironing. Save the iron for your cottons and linens.
- Dry clean all wool garments at the end of the wearing season. I advise storing them in muslin bags with herbal moth repellants. Moth balls are caustic and often don't do an effective job.
- If spaces are too small to store textiles flat, roll them rather than fold them. Cover them first with acid-free tissue before gently rolling, and cover the roll with more tissue.
- Heavily beaded or delicate silk garments should be stored flat, as should all textiles not in use. Acid-free boxes and tissue protect these fragile treasures best; these items may be found in archival supply catalogs. A less costly flat storage option is to line a drawer or box with a few layers of muslin. Pad the garment's folds with tissue, placing the lightest weight garments on top, with layers of tissue or muslin between.
- To safely hang vintage clothing, use padded hangers. Unbleached muslin covers (plain white cotton or linen) over the synthetic satin on hangers provide extra protection.
- If clip hangers are necessary for skirts, add several layers of muslin over the garment where it is to be clipped.
- Please, please, no metal or wood hangers for antiques!
- A rack of out-of-season vintage clothing is happiest when covered with a muslin sheet to protect against dust and harmful light rays.

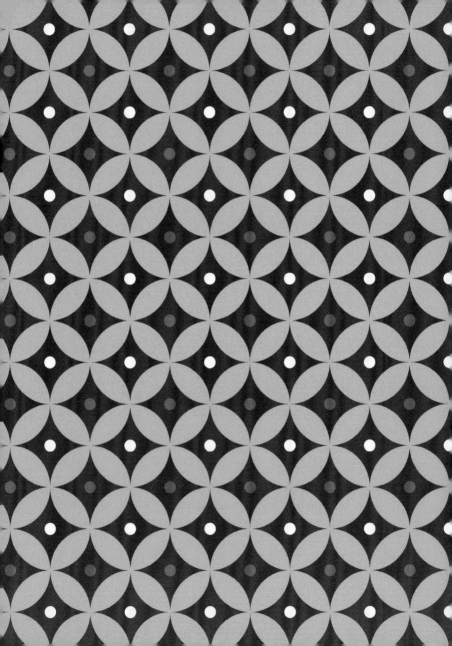

Chapter 8

Finishing Touches

CLOTHING FORMS ONLY A PORTION of the vintage fashion market. Equally abundant—and just as important—are the many categories of accessories: hats and hairpieces, shoes and handbags, costume jewelry, scarves, gloves, aprons, and on and on. Vintage accessories are a treasure trove for anyone with an eye for the unique seeking to enhance their wardrobe. Unusual materials, stunning craftsmanship, high quality—all hallmarks of embellishments from eras past—are a fabulous source of fashion inspiration. In this chapter, we'll focus on the essential tips and basic know-how that are sure to make your hunt for chic accessories a success.

All About Embellishment

ALMOST EVERY FLEA MARKET AND VINTAGE store offers accessories, with some dealers specializing exclusively in one category. Fashionistas have always loved to adorn themselves, and fortunately many vintage frills, trimmings, and toppers have held up extremely well over the years, making them plentiful on today's market. One of their greatest advantages is versatility, and size is seldom a factor. With so much to choose from, you can really think outside the box and explore some less sought-after categories. Some items that can instantly add interest to your style are pretty umbrellas, cute wallets, and travel cases and luggage, to name just a few. Every few years vintage rhinestone brooches seem to make a comeback, and a chic cloche-style hat will forever be in vogue. And don't forget vintage glasses. Since my high school years I've been turning to vintage for prescription eyewear. Once you know which types of frames a good optometrist can handle, you'll always have a pair of unique specs that will define your look. Of course, nonprescription vintage sunglasses are available everywhere and can be worn immediately.

Each of these categories could easily fill a book—and they have—but let's briefly tackle a few of the more popular ones, from head to toe.

Costume Jewelry

One of the first things customers look at is jewelry. And why not? The variety is endless—everything from Victorian to Mod, from classic to kooky—and the styles are as fresh today as they were when they were first worn. For in-the-know shoppers, usually the first question they ask is: Is it signed? A signed piece of jewelry is the equivalent of clothing with a designer label, and the name can greatly affect price. It's helpful to familiarize yourself with the important manufacturers; for example, a parure (set of matching pieces) signed by Elsa Schiaparelli is rare and will be costly, valued at $800 or more. Unless they are remarkable in some way, unsigned parures usually fetch a fraction of that price. Pieces that are signed by makers deemed less important, such as Sarah Coventry or Avon, will be valued modestly, sometimes not much more than unsigned pieces. But just because the name isn't considered valuable by some, don't walk away. If you like it, who cares who made it?

Better manufacturers usually translate into higher quality, but you can find some good bargains if you know how to spot quality without the designer name. Some things to look for are rhinestones that are prong set rather than glued; sturdy clasps and chains; knotting between beads; and better metals such as sterling silver, rolled gold, and gold filled. Brilliance and sharp facets on rhinestones and crystal beads are an indication of good craftsmanship, too. The finer the features, the better the quality, so be sure to examine the sharpness of detail work, like filigree or carving. Feel the weight of an item in your hand; cheaper metals and findings are often lightweight (although the opposite is true of early-century jewelry, which is usually very delicate). Once you've taken the time to study and notice the quality of several types of jewelry, you'll become quite good at spotting excellence. And if a designer name is not so important to you, you'll soon be able to pluck out the hidden gems from among the plethora of less-expensive choices.

Another problem to watch for is authenticity. Many older pieces, including Victorian, art nouveau, and deco designs, are highly desirable in today's market; they bring high prices thanks to their age and iconic beauty. Elements of their distinctive motifs have been copied over and again throughout the decades, and it's not always easy to distinguish a reproduction from an original—even we dealers are sometimes fooled. If you're looking to buy early costume jewelry, start out with established, reputable dealers until you get a feel for the real thing. There are also clues to look for. Older brooches tend to have a C clasp, meaning that they close with just a hook that doesn't have a locking mechanism. Patina, or aged surface appearance, is another good indication of age, which is why most dealers refrain from polishing these early pieces. Overall, experience is your best teacher. I suggest visiting the shops and observing the differences for yourself. And, as always, ask the owner or online dealer any question that will help you make an informed, comfortable, confident purchase. Most of us just love sharing information with our customers.

Condition Report

As with all vintage, costume jewelry has been braving the elements for years and may exhibit tell-tale blemishes. Some are permanent, but many can be remedied. Here are some common flaws and a few fixes to try.

Surface dust and dirt are often easily removed, but don't start scrubbing just yet! Keep in mind that dust is an abrasive; it can scratch metal and plated surfaces and even rhinestones too. To clean older pieces, gently brush with a dry, soft toothbrush; if you need to polish further, use a soft cloth. For caked-on dirt or oils, moisten a cotton swab with a mild cleaner like Windex. Dab the area, wait a few minutes for the dirt to loosen, and then rub gently with a cloth dampened with cleaner. Don't try to pick off the dirt since you might remove the plating as well. Finally, rub dry. *Gentle* is always the word to keep in mind. Also, never submerge or soak costume jewelry in water or cleaners. Moisture will become trapped under stones or in crevices and grooves, causing future damage.

Sometimes a material has surface damage that is more than skin deep. Discoloration on plastics and some natural materials (e.g., ivory, nut, wood, and bone), especially from skin oils, is permanent. Corrosion is common on metals and may or may not be fixable. One type is *verdigris*, which results in greenish spots, coating, or crust on metal and always signifies bigger problems. If it has appeared on chains, clasps, or prongs, they may be permanently weakened and may break with wear. Sometimes you can clean off verdigris with little consequence, but if it is severe, the damage will be noticeable and irreversible. To clean, use a soft cloth or cotton-tipped swab dipped in lemon juice and gently rub the affected area. (Some people advise using ketchup or vinegar in place of lemon juice; it's basically the acid in these items that does the trick.) When finished, wipe dry with a soft cloth.

Like verdigris, rust indicates further weakening of metal. Remove surface rust by rubbing gently with a soft, dry cloth. For deeper cleaning, I rub the spot with dry baking powder and a soft cloth. To remove the baking powder residue, I brush with a very soft, dry toothbrush. There are rust cleaners on the market, but they may be caustic and irreparably damage the piece. Be careful to test them first.

Mechanisms come with their own set of concerns, though most are small and easily dealt with. Sticky clasps can be fixed if they're not badly corroded. I have had good success by applying a tiny drop of WD-40 and waiting a few minutes before gently working the mechanism open and closed. Never force a sticky clasp—it could break. If clasps are broken or have extensive rust or verdigris, they should be replaced. Bent or loose clips on earrings can be fixed most of the time if all the parts are intact, but they need to be taken to a professional. Any jewelry repairer can quickly and easily tighten them for a nominal fee, and a lot of vintage dealers will do the task for you as well.

Rhinestones present their own particular set of problems. A rhinestone's brilliance comes from the reflection of light off the metallic coating on the back; exposure to moisture can oxidize the foil, causing it to lose its shine. Dull stones that have no sparkle are called *dead rhinestones*. There is no remedy for this condition aside from having the stone replaced. A dull stone here or there might blend in and not ruin the overall appearance of the piece, but you should expect to pay less for a flawed piece than for one in perfect condition.

For weak, broken, or stretched bead necklaces, any jewelry store that offers repair service can easily restring them. If the strand was originally knotted between the beads, you'll probably want a professional to do the job. To restring beads yourself, be sure to purchase the proper type of cord;

because regular string or thread will quickly stretch out, they cannot be used. Check your local craft store for materials, and inquire whether they offer short, inexpensive classes on bead stringing—many now do.

All in all, caring for your vintage jewelry collection has a few simple rules. Store pieces in a dry place, one that doesn't become too hot. Moisture causes corrosion and dulls rhinestones, and heat will loosen glued-in stones. To prevent scratching and tangles, don't stack items; rather, store them in layers, with a cloth in between (try old towels cut into pieces). Remove dirt and oils or makeup immediately using a cloth dampened with window cleaner (such as Windex), and then gently rub dry.

Hats

This category is close to my heart. Having been a hat maker in the 1980s, I have a great love for the craft and perceive hats as the most artistic of all the accessories. Until the 1970s, wearing a hat was considered essential to proper dress, and women paid well for their millinery. As a result, fine examples in every imaginable style are plentiful today in every type of vintage venue.

As a vintage dealer, one thing that has become clear to me is that there are "hat people" and "non-hat people." No amount of persuasion will convince a non-hat person to start sporting one, no matter the style. However, lots of women love vintage hats and want to wear them, but they're unsure how to pair them with modern clothing. The good news is that it's more about expression than proper dress. Little whimsies from the 1940s and '50s seem to be a perpetual favorite among young women, and they can be worn with just about anything, even jeans. Cloche styles from the 1920s are rare and delicate and therefore difficult to wear, but fortunately the style was revived in the 1960s and '70s. These later examples are far more durable and totally practical for winter wear. Berets look great on absolutely everyone. And fedoras never go out of style—from Marlene Dietrich to Jennifer Lopez, a woman in a fedora is always intriguing. Portrait hats, fancy straws, and even simple boaters are all perfect for a garden party or outdoor wedding. Create mystery with a turban, turn heads with a cacophony of flowers, celebrate prim with a pill box—the choices are truly endless.

When choosing a vintage hat, you should first consider whether it's in good shape, and then whether it fits. Finally, do you like the way it looks on *you*? Unlike their modern counterparts, vintage hats come in different distinct sizes. If purchasing online, you must know your head measurement and thus your hat size. First, measure all the way around your head in the center of your forehead (see illustration, *below*). Measure accurately because even a quarter inch can make a big difference in how a hat fits. For ladies, this measurement is your hat size; a measurement of 22 inches is considered medium, or average. (Men's hats are sized differently; check online for a conversion chart to determine sizes of a man's hat.) Online dealers should provide the inside ribbon measurement of the hat, which is the size. If they don't, ask for it.

Hats can be secured with bobby pins or, even better, an elastic that attaches to the inside band at either side. The elastic is placed under the hair in back of the head, anchoring the hat in place. Some older hats still have their original elastics, but if it's missing, tacking one in is easily done. Ask for millinery elastic at your local fabric store.

Almost all high-end designers have had their labels inside hats, and many even got their start in millinery. Halston and Adolfo were hat designers first, as was Chanel. Designer labels add value to hats, just as they do in clothing, but sometimes the most sought after names are not ones the average person would recognize. Bes-Ben, Howard Hodge, Gwenn Pennington, and Lilly Daché are just a few of the good labels in headwear to look for. Good quality is easy to recognize. The materials will be of the highest grade. Feel a felt—if it is soft and velvety, it is of better quality. Straw should be smooth and evenly woven (unless of course it is a novelty straw). With better millinery, glue is seldom used except to adhere feathers. Most decorative details are sewn on by hand.

The final judgment for buying a hat is made by looking in the mirror. Try it on different ways before making your decision. A hat can look completely different depending on how you angle it on the head. Try it on backward, too. There are no rules about how to wear a hat, except that you like the way it looks on you.

Condition Report

If paying retail, examine the hat very well, checking for discoloration, fading, holes, and tears. Be aware that discoloration and fading are permanent, as are moth holes that are more than surface deep. Torn netting should be removed—there is no repairing it. Deeply embedded dirt is almost impossible to clean. If you're at a flea market, you may still want to buy a hat if it has a few condition problems but a much lower price.

With a couple restoration tricks, you can easily revive a hopeless-looking chapeau. If the brim is wired and has lost its shape, simply smooth out the

line by pinching it all around between your thumb and four fingers (spread slightly). Crushed flowers, feathers, netting, ribbons, and bows will curl back into shape with a little steaming. A teakettle works fine—just watch your fingers and make sure the rest of the hat is held far from the burner. Be careful, however: Steaming can worsen glued-on decorations (feathers, in particular) that have become loose. I tack them back in place with Magna-Tac, a millinery glue that does not discolor. (I've also used Tacky Glue, which is easier to come by.) Steaming usually works to bring shape back to a felt or straw hat that has been crushed. Allow the steam to hit the material while turning the hat slowly and constantly. Steam the inside of the crown first, then the brim, and it should begin to relax back into its original shape. For stubborn areas, gently shape the freshly steamed area with your fingers. Once you've reshaped it, let the hat sit for a day before wearing it. Note: Before steaming any hat, be sure to brush it with a soft garment brush so that dirt doesn't sink into the fabric and soil it permanently.

Steaming can also help stretch a hat that's a bit too small. This trick works best on straws or felts. To do so, start with the inside of the crown, aiming most of the steam at the band of ribbon at the edge. Turn very slowly until you've steamed the entire band. If there is an outside ribbon, give that some steam, too. Gently pull the hat onto your head or, better still, place it on a hat block in your size. (These millinery shaping tools are available from vintage shops and online auctions.) It will feel tight at first, but as you keep it on, the band will relax and the hat will stretch to fit better. You need to wear the hat for at least an hour for the stretch to take—longer is better. Stretching a cloth-covered hat that has a buckram (stiffened fabric) base is trickier and should be done by a professional.

Shoes

Let's talk shoes. This greatest of fashion obsessions represents both the most and the least practical accessory we own. The purpose of these utilitarian objects is to cover and protect our feet, but for centuries shoemakers and designers have been engineering the form in ever-more creative ways. And though form may have followed function, it was seldom done at the expense of style. It's no surprise, then, that the parade of designs and the superior craftsmanship of vintage shoes provide a fabulous resource for those looking to stand out in style.

In recent years, the quality of shoes has diminished dramatically; a lot of contemporary footwear is slapped together with glue and cheap materials. The look may be cute, but the shoes tend to fall apart quickly and can be pretty uncomfortable to wear. Not so with vintage examples. In fact, there are so many excellent shoe companies of years past that I hesitate to name only a few. Aside from the most famous names, such as Ferragamo, there are the better department stores to look for, namely, Saks Fifth Avenue and I. Magnin. My all-time favorite vintage shoes are Troylings made in the 1950s. They are always beautiful to look at, not to mention well made *and* comfortable. Once you've donned a pair of vintage heels, you'll notice how they're so much more comfortable than their contemporary counterparts. That's because of proper construction and heel placement, which manufacturers nowadays seem to care about less and less.

When shopping for vintage shoes, ideally you should try them on. But purchasing over the internet is easy as long as you know how to determine size and fit. Older shoes are usually sized by width as well as length, unlike modern shoes, which are generally sized by length only (8, 8½, 9, and so forth). Found inside older shoes are usually letters and numbers. The letters stand for the width: "A" indicates a narrow width, but it's not the

narrowest—there are double- and triple-A widths, which are extremely narrow. "B" is considered average, and "C" and "D" are wide. More recent shoes will indicate width by an "M" (medium), "W" (wide), and "N" (narrow). To help

online buyers, merchants generally provide measurements as well as the letters and numbers inside the shoe, so knowing your foot measurements is an important tool. To determine length and width, use a tape measure to measure the sole of your foot (or a well-fitting shoe). Lay a tape measure across the widest part of the ball of the foot, and then do the same from toe to heel on the insole (inside), making sure the tape lies flat. Note that the

width of the shoe can be up to one-quarter inch *shorter* than that of your foot because of the way the foot is cradled within the shoe, but the length should be slightly *longer*. (I have a wide foot and have found that I can wear a narrower shoe if I go up one-half to one full size in length.) If you're considering

shoes with a pointed toe, the length should be quite a bit longer, up to an inch. To be on the safe side, though, check on the merchant's return policy.

Condition Report

There are a few flaws in footwear to be aware of. Cracked or weak leather—a common problem on much older shoes as well as those made from delicate leathers—is not mendable. Verdigris (see page 152) on buckles and grommets can

Craftsmanship of Vintage Shoes

JONATHAN WALFORD
THE FASHION HISTORY MUSEUM

Until the twentieth century, women's footwear was an invisible element of fashion. Hidden below floor-length skirts and petticoats, shoes of soft waxed and buffed leathers or silk brocades were secret pleasures enjoyed only by the wearer. When hemlines were raised, the shoe quickly became a fashion icon. It could be said that the golden age of shoe design began the moment hems began to rise and ended when they had gone as high as public decency allowed, from about 1915 to 1990. During this time, styles came and went with alacrity. Modern footwear did not lack for quality as long as the shoes continued to be forged under the tradition of master craftsmen, a thousand-year-old system whereby skilled shoemakers handed down trade secrets of construction and finishing to apprentices. The tradition of quality materials began to be displaced during the Second World War with the use of substitute materials and synthetics in the postwar era. Today, an appreciation of modern classics has brought almost every shoe style back into vogue. Those seeking vintage versions should appreciate their quality, for only a few of today's modern masters, namely Manolo Blahnik and Christian Louboutin, keep the tradition of quality shoe craftsmanship alive.

be cleaned gently if it is not severe. A lot of vintage high heels, especially stilettos, have worn, broken, or missing heel tips (the protective piece at the end). You may not notice until you wear the shoes and the pressure causes them to crumble. When the protective part is gone, the metal-spike portion of the heel is exposed and walking can begin to wear down the heel itself (not to mention what the metal tip does to wood floors!). The great news is that any decent cobbler or shoe-repair shop can replace the tips for just a few dollars. Dull leather and minor scratches are easily remedied with a good cleaning of saddle soap and a finishing polish. If a shoe's inside lining (known as the sock) is loose and curling up, just glue it down. I use rubber cement and wear the shoe for a little while, to fix it in place.

Handbags & Purses

Along with costume jewelry, handbags are the most popular vintage accessory on the market and boast quite a following among casual shoppers and seasoned collectors alike. Although the purpose of handbags and purses is simple, they have come to represent far more than simply toting around daily essentials. They can be a status symbol, like the famous Birkin bag by Hermès, or an extension of our inner selves—tidy and prim, glitzy and glam, artistic and free-spirited, practical and no-nonsense. Handbags are fashionable, useful, and omnipresent, and the contemporary market is flooded with cheap clones. The quest for something different, something well made yet still affordable, drives a lot of today's fashionistas to the vintage market.

Each decade of the twentieth century has its own signature styles. In Victorian times through the 1920s, handbags tended to be small, often merely purses that dangled from the wrist. Metal mesh, intricate beading, embroidery, and velvet were popular. Leathers were delicate and frames ornate. These early bags are beautiful and fragile, so examples in good condition are hard to come by and command high prices. They're best reserved for special occasions and make lovely evening bags. Clutch-style bags in varying sizes were popular in the 1930s, and ones with decorative clasps are especially sought by collectors. In the 1940s, handbags began to have structure—and it's the shapes that are most remarkable: ovals, rectangles, trapezoids, and spheres were common. Clutch bags grew to enormous sizes. Exotic skins like crocodile became the rage, Lucite and Bakelite were used for frames and handles, and fabrics were favored over traditional leather. Practical colors like black, brown, or beige were most common, but occasionally you'll find a bag in a beautiful hue. These are much rarer and generally sell for higher prices.

Structured bags continued through the 1950s and '60s, and novelty shapes and unusual materials were abundant. Some of my favorites from these years are the "telephone cord bags" made of brightly colored, coiled plastic. Carved Lucite bags are true works of art. Signed versions are highly sought by collectors, and names such as Wilardy, Llewellyn, or Dorset-Rex can fetch big prices. Fortunately, there are lots of unsigned examples that are really wonderful and affordable, too. Luxury materials were also popular, with rich brocades and carpetlike velvets among the favorites. Roberta di Camerino created her two-tone velvet Bagonghi bag in 1949 and went on to produce numerous other styles as well. An authentic Roberta di Camerino is valued in the hundreds of dollars, yet if a designer name is less important to you, there are lots of similar styles priced well below that amount. Handbags made before the 1970s are almost always good quality; they were sturdily constructed with quality frames and durable hardware. Linings were often a handsome faille fabric, with the best bags lined in leather or suede. My favorite vintage handbags were made by a New York company called Koret. The quality and attention to detail rival any other manufacturer, including Hermès, in my opinion. There are dozens of other good names to look for: Lewis, Coblentz, Bienen Davis, and Dorfan, to name a very few.

The bohemian movements in the 1960s and '70s sparked a trend for shoulder- and sack-type bags, and the structured purse lost favor. Decorative treatments included fringe and tooled leather, and needlework, canvas, patchwork, and quilted fabrics were the craze. The oversized clutch was revived (although it never really went away), and long shoulder straps became an added feature. Vintage handbags from these decades are fairly plentiful and tend to be well priced. In the 1980s an obsession for designer bags gripped the market. Although Hermès, Gucci, Chanel, and Louis Vuitton may not have been in the budget for most people, the names were all too familiar and soon a healthy market for designer fakes had cropped up. More affordable status bags were Coach, Dooney and Bourke, and Etienne Aigner. Designers once again started to have fun with shapes and colors, and lots of whimsical novelty bags from this decade are available today, to add that special touch to a retro look.

Condition Report

Unless a bag was never used, the lining will usually show some signs of wear. Pen and makeup marks are common and permanent, although as long as they don't mar the exterior, most of my customers don't mind them. Pay close attention to handles since they get the most wear, and make sure all the hardware is in working order, especially clasps and closures. Cracks in leather and broken hardware are irreparable, but for less serious blemishes there are several remedies you can try—and a little effort can have dramatic results. Clean and polish a leather bag the same way you would a pair of leather shoes: Wipe off dust with a soft cloth, clean with saddle soap, and polish with shoe polish in the same color as the leather. If the color is difficult to match, mink oil is a great substitute. Make sure to test an inconspicuous spot before applying any product because leathers will sometimes discolor with cleaning. If the edges of the bag are worn (a common problem), touch them up with a matching shoe dye and then polish. I also have a rainbow set of indelible markers to touch up bags of unusual shades. One of my favorite tricks I discovered quite by accident. Vinyl and patent-leather surfaces are dented quite easily. As a milliner, I used steam to shape hats, so one day I decided to see what effect it would have on a badly dented patent-leather purse. I held the purse over a steaming teakettle for just a couple seconds and the surface immediately smoothed out again. Since then, I have rescued countless bags this way, although unfortunately the trick doesn't work on true leather.

Scarves, Gloves & Aprons

Scarves are one of those accessories that never go out of style. The way they are worn may be affected by trends, but there has never been a time that I can recall when wearing a scarf was not considered in vogue. Around the head or the neck, tied at the waist or onto a handbag, these simple hemmed bits of fabric have a way of adding instant panache. Grace Kelly, who for some represents the epitome of midcentury style and beauty, is said to have worn her Hermès scarf as a sling when she had a broken arm.

Now that's chic!

Vintage scarves are plentiful today. As styles of clothing changed and women purged their wardrobes, they often hung onto their scarves, which were more easily adaptable to the latest fad. Most are made from beautiful silks, and some of the prints are pretty enough to frame. During the war years, rayon was favored instead, and these types now have a collectors' following. The "Holy Grail" of vintage scarves seems to be early Hermès examples. Such high-end designer names can be costly, but in general vintage scarves are affordably priced. Some favorites to look for are signature Vera scarves. Vera Neumann was a textile artist and a prolific designer whose company produced quality scarves throughout the midcentury years. Despite their fabulous designs and beautiful materials, prices for vintage Vera pieces tend to hover in the modest $20 to $40 range. Exceptional examples may be higher, but not by much. The nicest scarves have hand-rolled edges (hand-stitched), which helps the material to drape better. Common in years past, the practice of hand rolling is now reserved for only the most expensive scarves.

Caring for a vintage scarf has a couple of important rules. Many of them require dry cleaning because brightly colored dyes can run if washed. Test any scarf for colorfastness before attempting to hand wash. For small stains, try spot cleaning as you would any silk garment (for more information, see page 127). If you store folded scarves for long periods, certain dyes can bleed onto other materials; red and purple seem to be the worst offenders. Rolling them in acid-free tissue paper should protect against this problem.

Like hats, gloves were once considered a fashion necessity. Besides offering protection from the elements, gloves add a touch of feminine mystery to an outfit. The finest ones are pure elegance, fitting the hand like a second skin. A dozen pieces might be required to make a single glove, and minuscule stitching had to be absolutely perfect. Sadly, fine glovemaking has become a dying art, but that's why vintage examples are so special. You'll find beautiful, luxurious details added for interest, everything from cutwork and embroidery to topstitching and ribbing. Some of these embellishments could be quite flamboyant, such as the dramatic cuffs popular in the late 1930s. Materials range from the finest kidskins and suedes to lace, organza, and fine silk and cotton knits. If you cannot try on a pair of gloves, it's necessary to know your size. Most gloves have a size marked inside, so compare that number to gloves you usually wear. You can also measure your hand (see illustration, *below*) to determine proper fit. Leather gloves have a tendency to shrink over the years, especially if exposed to moisture, so store them in a dry place (but not too hot). Cloth and lace gloves can be gently hand washed, as can some leathers (just make sure they say "hand washable" on the inside). Fine gloves are an elegant accessory, but as someone who hails from New England, I am also a big fan of cozy mittens. Most thrift stores put

out a seasonal bin of winter gloves and mittens where you can find all kinds of fun styles and materials. Look for examples that show little wear and something you can easily clean (most knit mittens are washable by hand).

Of all the vintage available, I think aprons are the sweetest and most nostalgic. For me they conjure visions of cozy kitchens and home-baked goodies. Their practical purpose was to protect clothing from the spills and mishaps of daily homemaking, but to dispel the drudgery

of a chore-filled day, women turned their aprons into a creative expression. Early-century examples were usually plain white cotton or a simple print, but women often used their needlework skills to add ruffles, embroidery, or lace. As time went on, pretty patterns and fabrics took the place of plain materials. Around the 1940s the full wrap-around apron appeared. Most styles of wrap aprons provided front and back coverage. The longer ones look a bit like sleeveless house dresses and can easily double as fun sundresses. Beginning in the 1950s, when entertaining at home gained in popularity, hostess aprons became the rage. These fancy little numbers were more for show than for practicality, festooned as they were with flounces and frills. Sheer voiles, organzas, and even satins were used in place of easy-care cotton. Aprons make a great collection, and the fancy ones are fun to wear, particularly when hosting your own get-together. And there's still nothing like an old-fashioned full apron for preventing cooking spatters and spills from ruining your clothing. Most can easily be hand washed; just look out for set-in stains and tears. Best of all, they're plentiful on the vintage market, prices are reasonable, and the choices are endless.

THERE ARE FEW THINGS MORE FUN than shopping for vintage accessories— the market abounds with something for every wallet, every personality, and every style. You can also find these lovely finishing touches in antiques shops, at specialty shows, and on websites. Ideas for wearing them are limited only by your imagination. When I was a young girl, my mother used to fashion cute halter tops out of her old scarves for my sister and me to "sunbathe" in. So think creatively. Don't forget to look at knit shawls, which are a great way to keep warm and look chic at the same time. Cluster brooches and layer beads, or choose one fabulous piece to transform an outfit. Clip earrings have wonderful alternative uses: They make great shoe clips, or try fastening them to the neckline of a dress or sweater. A plain beret or felt hat is a common canvas for pins and brooches, but you can also dress up a plain clutch with the same. Try on, experiment!

Chapter 9

Altered States

FASHIONING NEW CLOTHES OUT OF old ones is nothing new. As long as people have been wearing clothing, they have been coming up with ways to reuse instead of discard. Call it what you will—restructuring, retro-fitting, refurbishing—the process is basically the same: little alterations that give outdated styles a more contemporary look. Today the shopping site Etsy overflows with whimsical wearables created by crafty innovators who lavish hours stitching and gluing bits salvaged from finds at the local thrift. Here are some ideas to kick start your creative rethinking of vintage clothing.

Reinventing the Past

THE RESTRUCTURING OF VINTAGE IS MET with opinions on all fronts. Many dealers and collectors work hard to restore vintage to its original state and strongly disapprove of permanently altering any garment. Other dealers seem to have little regard for preserving history, indiscriminately hacking off maxi dresses to sell as minis or cutting up 1930s bias slips and calling them camisoles. (Note: A reputable dealer always informs the customer of any alterations done to merchandise.) I am not a purist about preserving every last piece of vintage, but I do agree we should consider some important things before changing any garment. I would never take a scissor to a well-preserved 1930s garment because good examples from that decade are just too rare. History is woven into the charm of vintage, and pieces still in their original form are by far the most desirable.

Life is filled with exceptions, however, and sometimes it's perfectly acceptable to rework vintage to another end. Damaged pieces that are beyond repair, dime-a-dozen polyester prints, and loud muumuus would all run a greater risk of ending up in a landfill were it not for the ingenuity of crafty people who find good uses for clothing that "falls through the cracks." Sometimes the only thing you need to change is how you look at it! Here are a few ways to customize and modernize vintage garments.

Basic Projects

These projects require few sewing skills—and sometimes none at all!

From Skirt to Dress (or Top)

Vintage skirts with elastic waists are a gold mine for repurposing—they can easily be transformed into ultra-cool dresses or tops. The secret is to start with a skirt that has drape or fullness (or both) and enough length to fit over the bust and cover the torso, plus a bit more. The examples on the opposite page show you a few possible options. Wide elastic waistbands work best, but you can use a zippered waist if it fits around your chest. If you're worried about the top slipping down, use ribbons as shoulder ties. A few ways to attach them:

- Cut 4 pieces of ribbon long enough to tie (18 inches [45 cm] each should do). Tack 2 in front and 2 in back and tie at each shoulder.
- Measure the distance from the front to the back over each shoulder. Cut 2 pieces a little longer than that length (so there is something to sew to) and tack them in place.

- Sew 2 long pieces of ribbon onto the front only and tie around the neck, halter-style.

NOTE:

I always tack twice
for extra strength.

ALTERED STATES

Before

After

❋ 177 ❋

Underwear as Outerwear

Vintage lingerie can be breathtaking, and I have always thought it a shame to hide it beneath clothing. Others agree, and wearing underwear as outerwear is now too popular to qualify as a trend. This look *(below)* was created using a 1940s bias-cut rayon slip that has a sheer flounce and lace trim. Over top is a 1960s red half slip with black lace overlay. To pull the look together, a long black satin ribbon cinches the waist elegantly. Lingerie fabrics are thin, so think layers and variations on length. The mixture of colors and textures is exquisite!

Before | **After**

Advanced Projects

If your sewing skills are advanced, the possibilities for restructuring are endless. (Though I stress: Choose carefully. You don't want to destroy something that is now, or may someday be, historically significant.)

Dull to Chic

For clothing in good repair but whose dated details limit wearability, you can attempt a modernizing makeover, shortening length or removing sleeves.

To remove the sleeves, you can take the easy route: Cut away the material an inch (2.5 cm) from the armholes, roll it under (into the armhole), and hand stitch in place to create a finished edge. The professional way is to remove the sleeve entirely by carefully undoing the seam. Finish the open armhole with a matching strip bias-folded back and hand stitched in place. Add a ruffle to the bottom of a shortened dress to make it more modern and flirty. Ideally ruffles should be cut on a true bias (diagonal) and require a strip at least twice the length of the edge you are trimming. You may need to sew a few pieces together (though too many seams will interfere with the look). I often cut a ruffle from the edge of the original hem to get the longest possible pieces. If the fabric is not cut on the bias, interface the ruffle with stiff tulle. The result is a versatile special-occasion dress that retains its vintage charm.

To Repurpose a Vintage Piece of Apparel or Not?

ANNE COOK
OWNER, VINTAGEBAUBLES.COM

That is truly a question to which the answer is: It depends. Generally I'm not in favor of reworking vintage apparel, but sometimes it is justified and even desirable. When an otherwise outstanding, high-quality item is damaged, my first choice is always repair or restoration. Failing that, restructuring should be done with an eye to maintaining the designer's original intent (overall style and lines). The same is true with alterations for size. If the sizing is so far off that it's impossible, then the item should be left for someone who will fit into it better. Modifications that alter the designer's intent often fail, and what's left is a mish-mash of a garment.

Yet vintage is meant to be worn, and making something wearable may call for repurposing. Much depends on the item's existing integrity, that is, the quality of construction and fabric, historical significance of the styling, and the designer or maker. The rarer an item and the more representative of its era, the less likely I would be to alter it. For example, I would never remove a hip swag on a Ceil Chapman dress or shorten a 1950s Emma Domb ball gown, but I might re-hem an adorable 1970s maxi dress to street length. Would I remove a bust bow from a 1960s sheath dress? Maybe. (It would depend on how large the bow was and whether I could carry off the look well.) Not all vintage is great vintage, and if changing a hemline, sleeve length, or other style component makes you want to wear it, do it and don't feel guilty!

Examples of "important" vintage that should be preserved whenever possible:

1. Numbered couture
2. Iconic designer pieces, couture or ready-to-wear
3. Signature pieces by more obscure but fine designers whose work should be preserved due to its scarceness and quality (e.g., '40s/'50s Ben Barrack, '50s/'60s Bill Atkinson)
4. Quality pieces (labeled or not) that quintessentially represent a key style, era, or turning point in fashion (cutting-edge "New Look" pieces, early separates/sportswear)
5. Pieces that typify a style quirk or short-lived fad and may be difficult to find (e.g., a true late 1950s sack dress—not the shift dress that supposedly evolved from it and is omnipresent in vintage)

But please, unless you're an expert seamstress or tailor, have alterations done professionally. I've seen modifications that, had they been done well, could have really enhanced a garment. But being poorly executed, they merely ruined it. In short, repurposing should make sense and be well done!

Evaluating Vintage Shops

There are so many places to buy vintage nowadays: online shops, brick-and-mortar boutiques, vintage trade shows, thrift stores, and flea markets. Unfortunately, not all are equally reputable, honest, or user-friendly. Here are a few things to look out for before you make a purchase.

SHOPPING ONLINE

Buying vintage on the internet is convenient and there is a bounty of merchandise available, but you want to make sure you are buying from a reputable dealer. Online shops should:

- Have a clearly defined return policy.
- Present multiple, quality photos for each item along with a shot of the label (if there is one).
- Include a comprehensive description for each listing, citing fabric content, era of origin, accurate measurements, and condition.

Before purchasing from an online boutique or resale site:

- Read through customer reviews and testimonials.
- Read the dealer's mission statement or profile information. Look for dealers with experience and qualifications.
- Ask any questions you may have about the items directly. A good dealer will answer your questions quickly and graciously.

Because online shopping is so decentralized, prices can vary greatly. This means resale sites can be a great way to get a deal, but it also means you have to be especially alert to overcharging. When evaluating whether you're being charged a fair price:

- Consider typical costs for a garment of that era and type.
- Don't always jump at the lowest price. A lower price might mean additional costs or condition issues.
- Look closely at the photos and read the descriptions carefully to note any flaws.
- Make sure you factor in shipping—sometimes dealers who charge less make up for it with inflated shipping costs.

SHOPPING IN PERSON

Most dedicated vintage boutiques are run by expert buyers, but their pricing and quality may still vary. Here's how to evaluate any vintage shop you encounter:

- Make sure there is a place to try things on with a decent mirror; the absence of a mirror is a deal breaker.
- All items should be clearly priced with a brief description and ideally the era of origin as well.
- If there are any flaws to note, that should be written on the tag.
- Look for a posted return policy.
- I prefer places that separate out categories and don't jam the racks—that tells me the owner cares about their stock.
- Ask if the business guarantees the authenticity of high-priced, designer items and will fully refund any purchase that proves to be a fake.
- A note about cleanliness: use your nose. If the clothes are clean then the store should smell fresh. These same rules apply when you shop at a vintage trade show.

Shopping for vintage in thrift stores, flea markets, and rummage sales can get down and dirty—"buyer beware" would be my best advice. On the other hand, they can also be great fun if you like the art of the hunt. Keep the following in mind and you should be OK:

- First and foremost, do not overpay. These places offer little by way of amenities or expertise so prices should be a fraction of those in retail venues.
- Most thrift stores do not allow returns, nor do flea market dealers, and trying on items is not always an option, so bring your tape measure.
- If you spot something of interest, look for flaws very carefully and expect to clean whatever you buy.
- Be wary of dealers who over-hype their wares. If something sounds too good to be true it probably is.
- Go with your gut and bring this book for reference. You might just walk away with a treasure for a song.

Selected Bibliography

Nearly every major designer has a book or two (or more) devoted to their lives and accomplishments, and general books on fashion and style crowd the marketplace. Here are my favorites.

François Baudot, *Fashion: The Twentieth Century* (Universe). A treasure trove of 20th-century fashion history.

Paula Higgins and Lori Blaser, *A Passion for Purses, 1600–2005* (Schiffer). This one I don't have yet, but I've been told it is a fabulous resource.

Susan Langley, *Vintage Hats and Bonnets, 1770–1970* (Collector Books). Good all-around history of the hat. Lots of great pictures.

Caroline Rennolds Millbank, *New York Fashion: The Evolution of American Style* (Abrams). My absolute favorite, filled with history and commentary on 20th-century fashion from the New York scene.

Judith Miller, *DK Collector's Guides: Costume Jewelry* (Dorling Kindersley). Stunning photographs and decent text on the most important names in 20th-century costume jewelry. Price values are on the high side.

Georgina O'Hara Callan, *The Thames and Hudson Dictionary of Fashion and Fashion Designers* (Thames and Hudson). A wonderful sourcebook for novices as well as seasoned vintage buffs; chock full of concise definitions and histories for nearly every fashion term and all the major designers.

Jonathan Walford, *The Seductive Shoe* (Stewart, Tabori & Chang). *Everything* you could possibly want to know about the history of shoes and their place in fashion. Beautiful pictures.

The Dover Book Company publishes a number of fashion books in large paperback form that are inexpensive and fun to collect. I especially like their Everyday Fashion series ('20s, '30s & '50s), which use selected reproduction pages from Sears & Roebuck catalogues.

Index

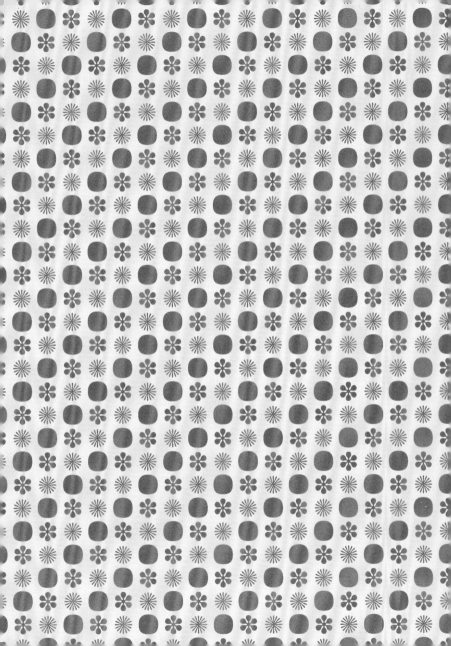

Acknowledgments

I would like to thank the following people for their help and support during the writing of this book. First and foremost, my wonderful husband, Bob, who gives without expecting. My sons, Peter, David, and Danny, and my daughter-in-law Kacey, thank you all for your sweet encouragement. My parents, who taught me that quitting is never an option. My good friend Kathy, who opened the door. Mary Ellen Wilson, my utterly amazing editor. All my friends and family who lovingly cheered me on, and finally a big thank you to the members of The Vintage Fashion Guild for tirelessly promoting knowledge and passion for vintage fashion.